Car Seat Conversations
The Secret Life of a Dad

Copyright © 2026 by Jon Woolley
All world rights reserved

No part of this book may be reproduced, stored in a retrieval system, or transmitted in any form or by any means electronic, mechanical, photocopy, recording or otherwise, without the prior consent of the publisher.

Mission Point Press

Published by Mission Point Press
MissionPointPress.com
PO Box 700028
Plymouth, MI 48170

Cover Illustration by: Joe Peck
Design: Mark Pate

Hardcover ISBN: 978-1-968761-19-6
Softcover ISBN: 978-1-968761-18-9
LCCN: Available upon request

Printed in the United States of America

THE SECRET LIFE OF A DAD

Jon Woolley

M·P·P
www.MissionPointPress.com

Table of Contents

Acknowledgments v
Introduction vi
Meet the Team 1
    Fur Baby 1
    Note to the Babysitter 24

Dad Versus 30
    Dad vs. Christmas Trees 30
    Dad vs. the Grocery Store 56
    Dad vs. the Hair Salon 77
    Dad vs. Disney 94

Kate (Almost) Kills Dad 130
    Kate Boot Camp 130
    Kate Born on the Bathroom Floor 133
    The Kate Workout 152
    Kate Kills Sleep 162
    Seven Reasons Why We Can't Have Another Kate 173
    Kate's Surprise Birthday Party 178

Claire Saves Dad 188
    And So It Begins 188
    The Game 206
    Gone Fishing 233
    Next Man Up 250

Author Bio 266

Acknowledgments

I would like to give special thanks to the people who encouraged me to write this book, especially my family. I would like to thank The Better Half: You gave me my daughters and so much more. I truly "married up" with you. To "Claire" and "Kate": You unwittingly provided the content. You make me want to be the dad you think I am. I love you both.

To Colleen, thank you for your unwavering support, and letting me marry your daughter.

To Justin, my podcast cohost, thank you for your encouragement. It kept me writing.

To Shelley, Josh, Danila, and John, your beta reads and words of affirmation helped get this book across the finish line.

Thank you, Joe Peck, for letting me borrow your artistic genius to create the cover.

Thank you Erin for fixing my social media sites. Also, thanks to Colleen T. for the author photos.

Lastly, special thanks to the Lord; He has given me gifts beyond measure.

Introduction

You are about to observe something very rare. It's not the dad; those are everywhere. You probably have one lounging around your house right now. It's not the kids; heaven knows those are impossible to avoid. If you're reading this in bed, there is a good chance that a small tuft of hair is going to go bobbing behind the footboard before you finish this sentence. No, it's the two interacting. The whispers into cupped hands that only a dad can decipher. The famous: "Don't tell Mom about this, ever." It's why there is chocolate milk between our floorboards and how two little girls learned where goldfish go after Dad's special "flushing funeral."

Thoreau once said, "Most men lead lives of quiet desperation and go to the grave with the song still in them." Thoreau never had children. If he did, he might have drowned himself in Walden Pond. I certainly have days of quiet desperation, but my two daughters have released my song. They are my love. And I shall go to my grave happy, with a hug from each of them. It is a delicate balance. But I hope our love for each other shines through as we pull back the veil on our secret world.

As a teacher married to a lawyer, much of the childcare naturally fell to me. Afternoons, holiday breaks, summers—I was the constant.

And through all that time together, a special bond grew between my daughters and me.

I've condensed and combined a few events, but everything you're about to read truly happened. Much of it was written down as it unfolded; the rest comes from my admittedly imperfect memory. Still, none of this is fiction—you couldn't make it up if you tried.

———

Claire puts her face right next to mine. Our eyeballs almost touching.

Claire: Me and you. We're a team.

Me: Being on your team is the best thing that ever happened to me. You saved me.

———

1
MEET THE TEAM

FUR BABY

Less than six months into our marriage, we (or rather I) decided to acquire a baby. A fur baby. Every marriage has the inevitable talk of children. And during this talk, past the smiles and nodding, both people have the unspoken fear that they would irreparably screw up any child they collectively bring into this world.

So, we (or rather I) decided to get a puppy. Better known as the "trial kid." I had come to the conclusion that this practice kid would make or break the possibility of real children.

I was determined to get a boxer. A big dog for a big guy. I knew nothing about dogs. The Better Half decided she didn't want a dog right now, certainly not a large dog, and definitely not one that would reside inside the house. I had a lot of battles to win. Back in her West

Virginia hometown, dogs were outside creatures, like pigs and cows. Not furry pillows to lie on while watching *Friends* reruns. I had to calmly explain that we lived in the suburb of a major city. No one else had a doghouse in the backyard, nor did we have twenty-five acres like her parents. What we did have was a busy four-lane road next to our house. I believe I argued this by calling her a "Confederate nutcase." It went as well as could be expected.

After weeks of calling her at work and interrupting something lawyers call "billable hours," she caved and told me I could get my boxer puppy. I bought dog supplies and even a book called *Boxers for Dummies*. The book was not very encouraging. Boxers were big, stubborn, and liked to jump on people. They had a flat snout that caused them to drool and snore. It said nothing about their love of being used as pillows while watching reruns of *Friends*, but that did not seem promising either. I was going to fail. Our dog would be horrible and end up in the pound like crazy Otis from *Lady and the Tramp*. We would never have children. This whole idea was backfiring.

One day, while watering a tree in our front yard, a tree that looked to be withering and dying, much like my chances of ever having wonderful well-adjusted children, a lady walked by with a beautiful white dog. The dog had no leash. With a simple wave of her hand, this mystical creature bounded up to me and nuzzled my hand.

The lady whistled, and it returned to her side. I chased her down the street like I was pursuing my last chance at offspring.

She said the dog was a new breed. A cross between a poodle and a golden retriever, known as a goldendoodle. I might have named it poo-triever. I thought of my manly boxer. This dog was the opposite. It was girly and passive. It didn't drool. It probably loved *Friends* reruns, and it resembled a fluffy pillow.

When I was single, on a whim, I bought a Jeep Wrangler. In memory, I loved it. It was loud, bumpy, cold, and broke down all the time. Daily, I hated it. Once married, I had to jettison the Jeep, and I inherited an old Ford Escort. It got forty miles to the gallon and ran like a charm. I stroked my chin.

This goldendoodle was a golden ticket. There was a good chance that even a rube like me could raise a decently behaved one. Then I could justify having kids. I got the breeder's contact information and ran in the house. The breeder recently had a litter of puppies. I could have the pick of the litter. Destiny. I called The Better Half and interrupted billable hours. I told her all about this new breed called goldendoodle and that we were getting one. She let me know that the promise of a dog was a partial win. I could get a dog, "just not right now." The date would be determined by her. I didn't mention that goldendoodle puppies cost $1,000. I was pretty sure the dogs back in West Virginia cost $25 and came with a free shotgun. I was crushed.

I had an idea. One we would look back on and laugh. Or she would hate me forever. Totally worth the risk. I called the breeder and made an appointment for that evening. I plotted out how my conversation would go with The Better Half. I settled in for a *Friends* rerun until I heard the garage door go up.

"Let's just drive and look at some puppies. We'll go out to eat on the way home. Puppy date night," I said.

"How big do these dogs get?"

"Like thirty-five pounds. Max," I answered in what could be called a half-truth. Since that was about half their size.

"We're just looking? Right?"

"Just looking. For the future," I said while tapping the blank check I had in the back pocket of my jeans.

We drove to a secluded farmhouse. Two beautiful amber golden retrievers came up to the car to greet us. An old lady took us up to the barn where she was keeping the puppies. She laid out a blanket, and six little balls of fur rolled over it like tiny tumbleweeds. The Better Half picked up a dark red girl and held her to the crook of her neck. She looked up at me, and I pulled the check out of my back pocket and started writing.

We picked out names over Bob Evans biscuits and gravy.

"I like Abby," said The Better Half.

"Me too."

"Hey, why did you have a blank check in your pocket?"

I was supposed to pick up my puppy at eight weeks old. I convinced a friend to get one from the same litter, and we decided to pick up our puppies at six weeks. We were both teachers and planned on spending our summer training puppies. Getting them early was like choosing to have a premature baby. But we didn't know that. Yet.

Five minutes into the ride home, they both puked all over the car. Luckily, I had borrowed The Better Half's Camry. I wouldn't want partially digested Puppy Chow all over my sweet 1993 Ford Escort.

After the pukefest, both dogs curled up next to each other and slept the rest of the way home. The other puppy was already wearing a Purdue collar, and my dog would love Ohio State. I decided that's why they puked; Big Ten rivalries run deep.

As soon as we walked in the house, Abby peed on the carpet, sprinted across the room, and fell flat on her face. I rushed to pick up my new baby and stepped in pee. It looked like she had died midstride. I assumed I had killed her already. I scooped her up into my arms. She was asleep.

I had inadvertently acquired a torture device. Abby was awake when she was supposed to be asleep and asleep when she was supposed to be awake. And now, so was I. The Better Half was busy working eighty hours a week. She was completely unaware of my new schedule. She assumed she had married a narcoleptic fool.

The Better Half would come home and eat dinner, and we would head right for bed. Within ten seconds, she was in a coma. Straight to Snoresville, population one. Then Abby would start crying in her cage. The Better Half wouldn't budge. I even tried clapping in her face. Nothing. Soon, Abby and I were jumping on the bed together with the radio on while sharing a bag of potato chips. All the while, The Better Half snored away. When The Better Half got up for work, Abby and I would be sound asleep. I can still feel her disappointed glare.

Abby slept in her cage for about an hour and a half at a time, peed herself, laid down in it, and cried like a baby. I set an alarm for hour-and-a-half increments. If the puppy woke before me, it was puppy-bath and clean-the-cage time. I don't know why the CIA ever got in trouble for torture. They could just give every captured terrorist a six-week-old puppy. In two weeks, they would tell you anything you would want to know. Trust me.

This puppy was about as much fun as a porcupine to a balloon. She bit me with little sharp teeth. All the time. I signed up for a puppy, not a baby T-rex. She didn't seem interested in *Friends* reruns at all.

Once, she snuck upstairs and got ahold of a potted plant. She ripped it to pieces and spread the dirt all over the guest bedroom. The Better Half had received a real Persian rug from an old boyfriend. Abby mistook it for a rawhide chew toy. The Better Half was livid when she got home. I wasn't too mad about the rug from an old boyfriend. But I did start to think getting this dog was a terrible mistake.

In a few long weeks, everything started to change. The sharp little teeth fell out. She tripled in size. She knew me. And I started to know her. We became an inseparable team.

We bonded on our daily walks. Abby was superior to so many of these other dumb dogs, and we both knew it. She would heel then sit as soon as I stopped walking. The lady down the street would be pulled past us by her dog. Abby would glance up at me with a soulful look as if to say, "Maybe if you didn't want your dog to pull, you shouldn't have bought a husky." I'd nod in agreement. We'd both smile. She'd smell the husky's butt, and we'd move on.

We would walk down to what some developer had deemed a park. Really, it was just a big field of grass. I would throw the Frisbee. Abby would snatch it right out of the air with these crazy Baryshnikov leaps. She would bring it almost all the way back to me. I'd have to chase her the last two feet while she deftly turned to the right and left before she would let me get it back. Soon, we were both exhausted.

She learned to sit and lay down in mere minutes. I taught her "stay" and "come" by playing hide-and-go-seek with her in the house. I'd command her to "stay" then go hide and yell "come." One time, she found me lying down in the bathtub. I can still see her snout poking through the shower curtain. We both had a good laugh over that one.

By the end of the summer, I had a true companion. I even moved that Persian rug downstairs in front of the couch. Abby slept on it every night. My goldendoodle had worked out.

Abby looked like a wimp, but strangely enough, sounded like a doberman. I had some men doing yard work while I was gone. Abby could hear them and had been barking incessantly inside the house. When I got home, the three guys begged me not to let out my attack dog. Once they saw Abby, we all had a good laugh. And Abby had kisses for every one of them.

Abby just kept growing. She was a lot bigger than the thirty-five pounds I had promised The Better Half. Almost twice that size. But The Better Half never held my half-truth against me, because she loved Abby as much as I did. Abby's hair would grow out until she looked like a red sheep dog. I'd get her shaved, and it was like we owned two different dogs. I joked she was half Chia Pet.

We took Abby everywhere, and everyone loved Abby. My brother and my boss both got goldendoodles. Now people were chasing me down the street to find out what kind of dog I had and how they could get one.

Our cleaning lady especially loved her. She cleaned while we were at work, and Abby would follow her all around the house. She would lie belly up next to the tub while the woman scrubbed it and climb up on the couch when she dusted the coffee table. Those big brown eyes hoped for one extra scratch before they both moved on to the next room. Sometimes, the cleaning lady would stop by on random days just to see Abby. I'd get home from work, and there would be a note, and Abby would be smiling as she chewed on a new bone.

The old lady next door hated animals. I tried to keep Abby out of her yard. Once I saw Abby trot toward her house. I ran outside to find Abby sitting just across my property line. She had crossed the underground fence and just took the shock. Old Ann was just standing there talking to her in a soft voice while stroking her head. I apologized and grabbed Abby's collar. Ann said she finally found someone who would listen to her problems. She wanted Abby to visit her every day from then on and would often bring her treats.

Then we had baby Claire and Abby got bumped down the totem pole, but she never registered a bit of complaint. Abby loved baby Claire like she was her own pup. She never once took one of her stuffed animals and ripped it to pieces, although I could tell she wanted to. And soon enough, little Claire was "accidentally" dropping half her food on the floor. Abby would lie belly up under her high chair, mouth gaping open, and wait for the inevitable rain of Cheerios.

I only saw Abby get angry once. I was walking baby Claire in her stroller. Abby was following right behind. A rottweiler and a German shepherd came running at us out of nowhere, teeth bared. I stepped in front of the stroller and prepared for the worst. I was shoved back, violently. By Abby. She growled, and the hair on her back stood up, making her look like a giant Chia Pet. The dogs backed off. Maybe there was a little wolf mixed into that poo-triever of mine.

I had heard that babies say "dada" first because the "da" sound is easier for them. Claire's first word was not "dada." It was "dog." I distinctly remember her mother and I going into her nursery in the morning, and baby Claire would already be standing in her crib. Claire would look right past our smiling faces. We would say in unison, "Good morning, baby girl!" She would answer, "Dog?" She did this every day. When my brother came to visit with his goldendoodle, Claire would go absolutely nuts in the morning. She believed, while she slept, her dog had somehow doubled.

Then we had baby Kate, and again, poor Abby slid down the totem pole of importance. Kate followed the same pattern as Claire. She said "dog" first and loved Abby with all her being. Who could blame her? Abby had thick red fur, the longest eyelashes ever seen, and big brown expressive eyes.

If anyone got sick, Abby would carefully cuddle with them on the couch. When I watched TV while lying on the floor, she would come up and bury her head in my shoulder and roll into a dog hug. And yes, she loved *Friends* reruns.

As the years went on, Abby didn't really need a leash anymore. She liked to be with her family and stayed where we were. She slept a lot. She still loved going for a ride in the car. No matter how many times I put her on the floor in the back seat, she always climbed up into the seat like a human and looked out the window. Every time I stopped at a light, the guy next to me would look over and be shocked to see a hairy figure staring back, smiling.

Abby rarely ran in those later years. No more acrobatic dives for the Frisbee. If I threw it, she trotted after it, then stopped halfway and looked back at me as if to say "Really?" The bunnies and birds once again invaded my backyard as Abby became more of an observer than a pursuer. Live and let live, that was her old dog motto. She liked to cuddle on the couch she wasn't supposed to be on. Claire and Kate still ate cheerios in the morning just so they could "accidently" drop a few for Abby.

One year, our family went out of town for Thanksgiving. We had to take a plane, so Abby stayed with my sister. This was fine with Abby. My nephews adored Abby, and she could count on them sneaking her some leftovers. That Friday, we received a call from my sister. Abby wouldn't eat. Not even a slice of turkey. She took Abby to our vet. He ran a few tests, but thought it was just a touch of dog flu.

When I got home, she ate some food and seemed to get better. Abby had never been sick, so she was probably due to catch a bug.

The Better Half took her back to the vet to make sure we had the right prescription.

The vet called that evening. I was standing in the front room, right next to Abby's Persian rug. The sun was setting through the plantation shutters, and the room looked like it was striped.

"I have some bad news. Abby has hemangiosarcoma, a very aggressive cancer, in her spleen. You might get a few more good days out of her, but she's going to go downhill pretty fast," said the vet.

I thanked him and hung up. I went into the kitchen, where Abby was sleeping on the floor. She heard me coming, and every part of her remained motionless except for that big furry tail. It slapped the hardwood floor. I put her head in my lap. She looked up at me and smiled. I swear it.

That night, in the darkness of our bedroom, The Better Half and I discussed the impending death of our first child. And for the first time in over a decade of marriage, I cried.

The next day, Abby seemed to return to her old self. She tried to roll in raccoon poop in the backyard and even head-faked a squirrel into thinking she was going to chase him. I bought her special organic canned dog food that had a per ounce price higher than sirloin.

I told Claire and Kate. They were devastated. Claire made a sign-up sheet for people to promise to pray for Abby. She took it to her first-grade multicultural classroom. When she brought it home, I saw the names of Hanul, Ujwala, Yusaki, and Lakshith. Abby would be getting prayers to every deity from Jesus to Buddha to Hello Kitty.

I came home from work to see the cleaning lady had visited. It was not her day to clean, but The Better Half had texted her. She left a note saying she just came to be with Abby one more time. To cry. On the counter, she had left a picture of Abby in a frame that said Best Dog Ever.

Abby and I met Old Ann at our property line. When I told her the news, she was visibly upset. Ann walked away saying, "Who will listen to my problems now?"

The next day was a tough one. Abby barely moved. She wouldn't eat. All of a sudden, in the evening, she became her old self. She ate half a can of the expensive dog food. I read that living things often get one last burst of energy, lucidity, and normalcy before the end. I mentally prepared for the worst.

I drove home from work the next day and primed myself to find Abby dead on the mud room floor. I stopped and picked up the girls from the sitter. I fought back tears while explaining what we would find to the little girls in car seats behind me.

I slowly opened the entry door from the garage. There stood Abby, tail wagging and panting with excitement. A ritual that I had taken for granted until now. Her legs suddenly gave out, and she crashed to the floor. I scooped her up in my arms, just like the day

I brought her home as a six-week-old puppy. She had lost a lot of weight, and I could feel her ribs.

I laid her on a blanket in the living room and called her mom at work so she could rush home. I called the vet. He warned me of the possibility of a stroke or seizure. I had each of the girls say goodbye. Abby, with great effort, lifted her head so she could look each one in the eye. I had the girls retreat to their bedroom in case things got ugly.

A friend arrived to watch the girls just as The Better Half pulled into the driveway. I carried Abby, rolled up in the blanket, out to the minivan. She was dead weight. I shoved the bench seats back and laid Abby down in the space created. Abby's tail started wagging, slapping everything. She still loved car rides. And we both knew this would be her last. I shut the sliding minivan door and climbed in the front seat for the short drive to the vet. As I put it in reverse, I heard some fumbling and a groan from behind my seat. I was sure Abby was having a seizure. A smiling head popped up in my rearview mirror. I turned to see Abby sitting in the back seat like a person. It was her last car ride, and she was not going to do it lying on the floor. I put the window down a little, and she stuck her snout out.

Abby was still smiling out the window when we pulled up to the vet. I slid open the door and reached in to carry her. Her back stiffened. She hopped to the floor of the van and stumbled out. Every step was shaky, but it was her own. The vet had graciously set up a room, and we went right in. Abby collapsed on the tile floor.

The vet, a dark-haired man in his forties, came in and gave us each a hug. He pulled a syringe full of a bright pink liquid out of his coat pocket. It looked like Abby was going to be injected with bubble gum. I carefully lifted her up on the exam table.

While he gave the injection, I held her head in my hands and looked right into her eyes. For a brief moment, I saw the puppy I tricked her mom into buying. I saw the time I walked into the dining room for dinner to find her sitting like a person at the table as my girls laughed uproariously. I saw her jumping and catching a Frisbee, time and time again. I saw her collapsing on my chest in the dog version of a hug. I saw how excited she was every time I came through the door, even if I had just left to get something out of the garage.

Then the light in her eyes faded. She was gone. And so was part of me.

The day I turned 42, I decided to make a change in my life. I started waking up at 4:30 in the morning to pray.

I'm well-versed in theology. Theologians say that only humans have souls that continue past this present world. Animals just die. Dust to dust. I have prayerfully decided those theologians can go to

Hades. When I die, there will be a red dog there to welcome me. Her tail will be wagging like never before.

So, toss a Frisbee in my casket. I'm going to need it.

Kate: Dad, your face needs something new. Something to make it pop.

Me: Is that right?

Kate: You ever think of wearing lipstick?

I took the girls to a free magic show at the library. There were thirty-six moms there and me. I counted. The magician pulled quarters from ears and made a tennis ball vanish. He was really good. At one point, he pulled some tighty whitey men's underwear out of a hat. Every kid in the audience turned and looked at me.

Claire (whispering): Dad, did you see that? He has your underwear.

Me: Those are not mine.

Claire: You better check when you get home. I bet you're not wearing underwear now.

Me: Just watch the show. I already checked.

I roll over to find Claire staring at me at 1:47 a.m.

Me: I thought we talked about this. You scare Daddy sometimes at night.

Claire: I can't sleep.

Me: Why?

Claire: My lips are chapped. I need to sleep with you.

Me: I see you are carrying a magic wand and a play doctor kit.

Claire: You never know what you are going to see when you get out of bed. I like to be prepared.

At our local grocery store, there is an old guy with white hair and a beard manning the middle lane. Little Claire leans out of the cart, grabs my head, and pulls me close. She looks deep in my eyes. She whispers, "You make sure we check out with Santa."

Kate: I got my costume all ready for dress-up night at church. Grandma helped me make a new costume. You're going to love it.

Me: I know you wanted to wear the wicked witch costume, but that would have been offensive to some people at church. Did you choose something from the Bible instead?

Kate: I'm Jesus. Jesus Christ.

Me: Do you still have the witch costume?

Claire: I saw this thing on TV where, instead of rubbing people's backs, this lady was karate chopping.

Me: Let me guess. You want to karate chop my back.

Claire: You will love it. You know why?

Me: Why?

Claire: I'm a ninja.

Kate: How do people make up jokes?

Me: Well, they may use rhyming words or say something that everyone knows is not true. Stuff like that.

Kate: You look very handsome today.

Me: Thank you.

Kate: Joke.

Me: Claire, before we go to Grandma's house, I have some bad news. Remember how she had those two black cats that you loved to play with?

Claire: Yes.

Me: Well, there was a terrible accident. And one of them died.

Claire: One is dead?

Me: Yes.

Claire: Okay, Kate can play with that one.

———

Car Seat Conversation on the way to drop off the girls at the sitter at 6:45 a.m.

Claire: Dad, I smell something. Did you toot?

Me: Nope. Probably a skunk.

Claire: There sure are lots of skunks on the way to Lisa's in the morning.

Me: Maybe the skunks need to eat less chili.

———

Kate: The teacher said that, for career day at school, we can dress up for what we will be when we grow up. I will need a black cape and a lightsaber.

Me: You are not dressing up as Darth Vader.

Kate: Fine. Help me find my gown and crown. I'll have to go as a boring queen.

———

Me: You missed school yesterday. You get all caught up?

Claire: Oh yeah. Some kid tried to do a backflip off the bench and totally broke his arm. Billy was cussing like crazy. Too bad a teacher was behind him. Busted. Joe likes Mary. She doesn't like him. All caught up.

Me: Schoolwork. Caught up on schoolwork.

Me: I'm sorry I forgot to pack your lunch today for school and you had to pack your own.

Kate: You ever had a Nutella sandwich with gummy bears?

Me: I never even heard of one.

Kate: Well ... it's delicious.

Claire: Having two grandmas is confusing. I have been thinking of ways to tell them apart.

Me: Really.

Claire: Well, one has black hair and one has white hair. The one with black hair I've decided to start calling black grandma.

Me: No. That is not appropriate. You do not have a black grandma.

Claire: I'm going to call her black grandma.

Me: No. You are not. And we are going to have a long talk about why not. You are going to have to get sensitivity training to keep your job here as The 5-Year-Old.

Claire was watching me dump bags of candy in a bowl to prepare for Trick or Treat.

Me: Don't touch this candy. I'm going to hand it out to the kids tonight.

Claire: Well, I'm going to come to this house for sure.

Me: You can't trick or treat your own house.

Claire: I can.

Me: I won't give you any candy.

Claire: You won't even know it's me. I'll be wearing a costume. Do you even know how this thing works?

―――――――

When I pick up Claire from preschool day camp, I have to present a state-issued ID with my picture on it. Leading to this conversation while walking to the car:

Claire: Dad, do they make you show your driver's license, so they know you pick up the right little kid?

Me: Something like that.

Claire: Yeah, because you could get home and say, "Come here, Claire." And the kid would say, "I'm Jeff."

―――――――

Claire: Christmas is only three months away! We should start being on our best behavior now, for Santa.

Me: That's a good idea.

Kate: That is about the dumbest idea I ever heard.

———————

Claire's prayer tonight:

Dear God,

>Thank you for the team of me and Daddy. Please help Mommy learn to tell jokes and be funny, so someday she could be on our team.

Amen.

NOTE TO THE BABYSITTER

Dear Amy,

Thanks so much for coming over tonight. I hope your last year of college is going well. I apologize for the length of this note, but there are a lot of items to go over regarding the care of my two girls. Kate is four, and Claire is seven. First of all, the little one might try to kill you. Just kidding, nothing so serious in this note. But seriously, stay vigilant.

Dinner: I set out mac and cheese, hot dogs, and peas. Simply make the mac and cheese according to the directions on the box. While you are making it, the little one will push a chair over and try to help you. You won't see her doing this. She will just appear next to you, grabbing the spatula. She's a little creeper. Don't let her add the milk or butter. I've been a witness to her dumping half a gallon of milk into the pan. Don't let her stir, or food will be tossed across the room as though off a catapult. Cook the hot dogs in water on the stove, not in the microwave. They can taste the difference.

You say the blessing, unless you want a forever prayer where Kate names everything she can think of. And she can think of a lot of things. You dispense the ketchup. If it touches anything, even items that will later be dipped in ketchup, those items will be considered "ruined." They both love ketchup but hate tomatoes. Do not mention that ketchup comes from tomatoes. It will start this whole thing; trust me.

If they eat half of the peas and half end up on the floor, that is totally acceptable. Kate will try to eat her peas with her hands. Let her. Using a fork will take all night. They both get water to drink with dinner despite their insistence that they both get chocolate milk with every meal and Claire's claim of being calcium deficient. Kate will claim that I give her soda all the time. That is a lie. I once gave her a sip of Coca-Cola, thinking she would hate it. She loved it, and I have regretted it ever since. Use disposable everything. Clean up by throwing it all away. We want to save the planet, but your sanity is too high of a price to pay.

During dinner, Claire will decide she has to poop. She must ask to be excused. This will extend dinner by at least half an hour. There are to be no burping contests. Kate will be staring at Claire for any signs of her chewing without keeping her lips perfectly sealed. She will then report to you that Claire is not "chewing like a princess" despite the fact that Kate is reporting this with a mouth full of food. The dog will clean up the floor, except for the peas. If they are still hungry, they can each have a yogurt that comes in a tube. Do not let Kate open her own as evidenced by the yogurt stains on the ceiling above her seat.

Rules: No getting naked until bath time. Also, no putting on all the clothes you own at once. The little one cannot just throw her hands up and yell "freeze" to get out of trouble. Claire is not allowed to gather all the blank paper in the house in order to "publish" her own book.

No feeding the turtle or the goldfish all their food at once. The ant farm stays sealed despite claims that the ants want to "come out and play." No building obstacle courses for the dog that include life-threatening hurdles.

The couch is not a trampoline. No false mysteries that begin with Claire finding a post-it she wrote and declaring it a "clue." It ends with post-its all over the house and Claire claiming a reward of candy.

No screaming or screeching. But it should never be silent for more that fifteen seconds. No using the dog, jump rope, and the plastic snow sled from the garage to create a dog sled in the kitchen. If the toilet gets clogged from Kate using a ridiculous amount of toilet paper, she is to report it is stopped up, not float her bath toys in it.

No riding bikes inside. No teaching the dog piano, although her jazz ensemble is pretty good. No wearing capes. This leads to the belief that one can fly, which leads to four stitches in Claire's chin. If Kate attacks you with her lightsaber, just go with it. But you are not expected to go the rest of the night without using your arms because they are "chopped off by Darth Vader." It is impossible to do bath using only your feet. Trust me.

Bath Time: This is also known as "make a deal" time. I have placed two pieces of candy in the cabinet next to the bowls. Put them in the middle of the dining room table. Tell the girls that they don't get a piece of candy until BOTH of them are done with bath, clad in pajamas, and hair is brushed. If you try to punish Kate for not completing these tasks, Claire will feel guilty and not take her candy either. Then Kate will argue that she should eat Claire's candy, since no one is eating it, and it shouldn't just go to waste. This seems to make sense. And somehow, Kate ends up eating candy while standing in the kitchen wet and naked. Don't fall for her Jedi mind tricks.

When they get up to their room, have them take off their clothes and put them in the hamper. Claire will try to blast music and turn it into a dance party. Remind her of the talk she had with her daddy about girls who dance to loud music while taking off their clothes. The girls are to lay out pajamas, not Halloween costumes. Claire is not sleeping as a scary clown. Again.

Fill the bathtub with lukewarm water that they will swear is scalding hot. Don't forget about displacement; by that I mean the movement of the water due to two little girls cannonballing into it. Claire is not to wear a swimsuit or swim goggles.

When they get out of the bathtub, be wary of them calling the dog. The dog is not to be used as a towel. Immediately after stepping out, they will feel cold and crouch down. You have four minutes where they don't really move a lot. Enjoy.

Despite what Kate declares, it is not "backwards PJ night." Due to inherited genetics (from her mother), Claire wears some kind of orthodontic headgear that resembles a rat trap. Good luck putting that on. Have them brush their hair. Give them the candy then have them brush their teeth. Rinse the fist-sized green glob of toothpaste that Kate squirted into her sink down the drain like it is money. It is. Congratulations. Bath time is over.

Bed Time: Tuck them both into bed. Wait twenty seconds. They will both get up for last potty and drinks. Tuck them in again. Both girls say a prayer. Remind Kate to keep it appropriate. God does not have stinky feet.

Next, you tell them a story. They will name random objects, and you must include them in the story. Princess Pee-Pee should not appear in the story. Turn out the light. Kate will come downstairs in eight minutes, claiming her covers are messed up and she cannot get them back to "perfect." I don't know where she gets this obsessive-compulsive behavior (her mom). Then Claire will get up, claiming that Kate is humming (she is). Then Kate will get up and claim she had a terrible nightmare. She will describe said nightmare in great detail despite the fact you left her room thirty seconds ago. Hug it out but resist the urge to crush her. That should be it. Kate doesn't get up again until 3 a.m., and we should be home by then if we haven't decided to start a new life in Canada.

Feel free to watch TV. You will probably end up standing in front of the fridge with the door wide open as you contemplate what will repress the memories of the night. Let me save you the time. In the freezer, there is a box of frozen pot pies, but there's not. It's actually full of Reese's Peanut Butter Cups.

We pay ten dollars an hour. I left thirty dollars on the table as we should be gone three hours. Actually, I left forty dollars. I left sixty dollars on the table. Please let us escape again one day.

Thank You,
Dad

And on that Easter morning, a grand compromise was struck. Easter dress for Darth Vader boots.

2
DAD VERSUS

DAD VS. CHRISTMAS TREES

Throughout childhood, as I got bigger in stature, the artificial Christmas trees my mother procured got smaller. By the time I was in college, I would come home to a two-foot specimen perched on top of an antique sewing machine. Unbeknownst to me, my future wife was having the opposite experience. Her live trees were getting bigger and more luxurious by the year.

Three months into our marriage, my new bride instructed me to go get a large, live Christmas tree. I argued for a small artificial, but it was useless. We were going to recreate her childhood, not mine.

The early December air nipped at my nose as I unlocked my 1993 Ford Escort. I had started the marriage with a black Jeep Wrangler. I was trending toward bigger Christmas trees and smaller cars.

If this continued, soon we'd be decorating the massive spruce in our backyard, and I'd be riding a bike to work.

A few blocks away, at Walmart, a semi-trailer was parked at an angle in the far corner of the lot. Standing next to the trailer like an extended police lineup were about fifty trees. Having never purchased a tree of any type, I was amazed at the diversity in both species and price. From pines to firs to scotches, they all looked the same to me. Trees ranged from fifty dollars to over three hundred. I pictured myself dragging a wad of money to the curb in a few weeks, bound for the city's wood chipper. And I was certain whichever tree I chose, it would be the wrong one. I went for tall and cheap. Just like my new bride did in picking me.

A man in his late twenties walked over to me. I was the only shopper. He wore a stocking cap with a fuzzy ball on top and a dirty sweatshirt proclaiming a professional football team the world champions, who I am certain never won anything. It was the clothing I thought we sent to Third World countries. I was inspecting a fifty-eight-dollar fir.

"That one will work," he said.

By "work" I hoped he meant good enough that your wife doesn't punch you in the face. It looked plenty tall enough but a little skinny.

"I'll take it," I said.

The friendly seasonal employee bent over and grabbed one of the lower branches and proceeded to drag the helpless tree back behind the semi-trailer. He slapped the tree down on a pair of saw horses, and his chainsaw roared to life. He glanced up at me and must have seen the "What the heck are you doing?" look on my face.

"Ya gotta give em a fresh cut. A fresh cut is the key," he yelled. "Sap chunks up on your stump, and she can't get a drop of water in."

He sliced an inch off the end of the trunk and then, with one motion, he shoved the tree through a metal hole and it popped out the other side covered in what appeared to be a fishnet stocking. He grabbed it with both hands and lifted it over his head like a wrestler preparing for a body slam.

"You the Ford?"

He slapped it on top of my red Escort and tied it with baler twine. He used a combination of knots I could never hope to replicate. Did this guy have a past life as a wrestler/sailor?

"That won't go nowhere. You just pull that loose end," he said, flipping a piece of twine with his fingers.

"I just pull this string and all the twine and knots will come right off?" I asked, not expecting a magic trick with the purchase of a tree.

"Yep."

I arrived home triumphant and expected to find a thankful wife.

"How much was it?" she asked as soon as I walked through the door.

"Fifty-eight," I answered proudly.

"Fifty-eight! The tree farm down the road from my parents doesn't sell a tree over fifteen dollars. I cannot believe you wasted money like that."

I calmly explained that buying a live, but soon to be dead, tree was by definition a waste of money. And that we did not live in the backwoods of West Virginia. We were going to have to pay big city prices, and if she wanted to drive the seven hours to her red neck of the woods to get a tree, I would not stop her. And, by the way, it was probably scratching the roof of my Escort, a car that started out humiliating but one that I'd become quite fond of.

I stormed out into the chilly night. Pulling on that loose end of twine did indeed make all of it fall to the ground like magic. I grabbed the tree, and it immediately scratched my hands in self-defense. I tried to hoist it over my head but had to settle with the tip dragging on the ground all the way to the front door. I slammed it on the linoleum kitchen floor and collapsed on the couch while The Better Half put together the tree stand.

Without saying a word, we worked together to position our first Christmas tree in the corner of the living room. I dragged the tree next to her. She knelt down and loosened the four giant screws that twisted into the trunk of the tree. It's bad enough that this poor tree had to get chopped down, put in the back of a semi with no water, sold in a parking lot, and given a "fresh cut" before getting magically tied to the top of my car. Now it had to get four screws bored into its trunk and be crucified unto death in our living room for the next four weeks.

"Alright, drop it in and straighten it up!" she yelled.

We both heard a loud scratching sound like a cat sharpening its claws on drapes. We didn't have a cat. I hate cats. But not as much as I was about to hate our first Christmas. The Better Half looked at the ceiling, and then looked at me with a hate that burned of a thousand suns.

"You bought a tree that is too tall. And now we have a permanent green streak on our white ceiling. Nice."

"I will fix this tree," I answered with no plan in place as to how. I had a strong feeling she knew this. I had not accounted for the height of the tree stand in my mental math. The Better Half stared at me, then she turned away, perhaps realizing that if I had married up, she had married down since we both couldn't be the up.

"Strap it back on your car and have them cut another four inches off," she stated, as though that were an option. I couldn't lift the tree up onto the car. I didn't know how to tie it back on. And I didn't want more scratches on the roof of my car. I decided to solve this problem like a man. In an incredibly stupid way.

I hopped in my Escort and drove right back to where they were selling those trees in the Walmart parking lot. I marched into Walmart and speed-walked to the tools. I grabbed the first saw I found and headed home. I pick saws like I pick Christmas trees; they all look the same, and I know I'll get the wrong one. I was ready to give that tree another "fresh cut."

I stormed through the front door and jerked the tree out of the stand, spraying needles everywhere. I laid the tree down with half of it in the living room and the stump sticking over linoleum in the kitchen. I ripped open the packaging on my new saw and went to it. I sawed. And sawed. Sweat was dripping down my face. Every time I propelled the saw forward, a few needles were shaken off the tree. Finally, my arm aching, I pulled back to inspect my work. I had barely made it past the bark. I leaned back, wiped sweat from my brow, and The Better Half picked up the packaging I had thrown on the floor.

"Did you know you bought a saw made for cutting plastic PVC pipes?"

"I do now."

Whether male pride or plain old stupidity, I was determined to cut through the trunk of that Christmas tree. I removed my sweatshirt, placed my right hand on the trunk of the quivering tree, and went to sawing. The Better Half sat down on the couch and exhaled loudly as she turned on the TV. By the time she was halfway through some home repair episode where a man was using an electric saw to cut a wall out of a house, I was halfway through that trunk. And ready to pass out. Male stubbornness carried me through.

The Better Half and I worked in concert to put our decidedly skinnier tree back up. I went upstairs to shower while she decorated it and cleaned up the room. We had bought a new Dyson vacuum after our wedding. Turns out they do lose suction, when stuffed full of needles and sap.

I came down to a beautiful tree. It looked and smelled great. The strands of lights twinkled, and the bulbs filled in any bare spots. I carefully placed the star at the top. Then I filled the tree stand to the tippy top with water. We went to bed.

The next morning, The Better Half got a big glass of water and crawled under the bottom branches.

"We got a problem. This is still completely full of water. It hasn't taken in a drop."

She groaned and started to remove the ornaments and lights. I silently walked down the basement steps to where I kept the three, now four, tools I owned.

"You're not going to go get a new saw?" she yelled down after me.

I didn't even respond. I had a saw. And this tree was about to get another "fresh cut."

I learned that, after Christmas Day, they basically give away the tree I had bought and just about give away artificial trees too. Preparing for next year's fight, I bought The Better Half a 7.5-foot pre-lit artificial Douglas fir. It is the best Chinese-made fire hazard money can buy. I also bought her two other smaller artificial trees, one for the front window and one for wherever she dang well pleased.

"These three trees will be what our house uses! No need for a live one," I declared.

And every year since, we've had four trees.

Children, like Christmas trees, have a tendency to multiply unexpectedly. And they cost way more than you thought reasonable. Soon, I went from zero to two. From an early age, they would point to the green streak on the ceiling or pull a petrified needle out of the carpet, and they would inquire how it got there.

"Santa gets clumsy sometimes. Too many sugar cookies in one night," I'd say, laughing at my own joke while my daughter, Claire, stood there scratching her head.

I remember the Saturday afternoon when it all went sideways. Or more sideways. It was early December. It had just rained, and the sky was still overcast. A cold front had moved in, not cold enough to freeze the mud, but cold enough to make your nose drip. I was nestled into the corner of our sectional sofa with a blanket. Fire in the fireplace. Football game I could care less about on mute. Naptime.

I felt a dark presence enter the living room. I heard her say the words "family time" and that the ad said, "Dogs welcome." I pulled a throw pillow over my head. The Better Half dropped the big one: Christmas Tree Farm.

I went up to our bedroom. In the back of my closet, I had hidden an item in preparation for this day. I had purchased it years ago, hoping I would never need it. I put on a plaid, red and black, lumberjack shirt. If she was going to make me chop down some defenseless tree, I was going to look the part. Straight Paul Bunyan. I would not go quiet into that dark night.

My Ford Escort had somehow morphed into a family-friendly SUV, with a tree ready roof rack. For some reason, there was this rush to leave, as though the place was going to run out of overpriced trees. The Better Half threw the girls in their car seats while I gave our fat goldendoodle a boost up into the back hatch. Where she stayed for ten seconds before hurdling the back seat and joining the girls.

After a forty-five-minute drive, we finally saw a sign for the "Christmas Tree Farm." Which is not a farm at all, rather the giant side yard next to someone's country house with trees planted in rows. The Better Half was ecstatic. I was less so.

I parked in a line of a dozen cars and stepped out. My boots sunk into mud. I could see my breath. The Better Half got the girls out of their seats while I tried to corral the dog. I slipped on Abby's choke chain. It is supposed to choke her if she pulls on the leash too hard. Either it doesn't work, or my dog doesn't breathe.

"Where is Kate's coat?" The Better Half yelled.

"Probably at our house. We better go get it," I answered without a hint of sarcasm.

"I'll just hold her close. It will be fine."

"Make sure to keep an arm free, so you can chop down a tree."

We traipsed through the muddy parking lot to a plywood shack. It was heated by two old-fashioned space heaters with exposed bright red coils. Seemed like a fire hazard. The people running this operation must not have been very bright, but then again, I was here to pay more for a Christmas tree that I'd chop down myself. The only purpose of the shack seemed to be to keep the chubby lady who ran the credit card machine toasty. She smiled at me and pulled out a plate of sugar cookies.

"Would you two angels like a cookie?" she whispered to my daughters, clearly unaware that the little one was the opposite of an angel.

I knew those cookies. They were sold at Walmart. The same Walmart that had a parking lot in which I should have been buying my tree. The cookies were a decoy, so I forgot I was getting ripped off. Like when you are buying a car and the salesman offers you a free tank of gas if you buy right now.

She turned to me and shoves a heavy bow-shaped saw into my hand. I inspected it carefully. So, this was what they used to cut through the trunk of a Christmas tree? I handed it to The Better Half.

"I'm supposed to hold Kate and chop down a tree, Paul Bunyan?" she asked.

"I only use saws meant for cutting plastic PVC pipes. This would be too easy."

A man pulled up in a small tractor with a hay wagon attached. He had the appearance of a seasonal employee or homeless person. But the way he was smiling and joking as people climbed into the hay wagon made me think he owned the place. As we bumped along to the end of his yard, we all started to shiver, and Kate's lips turned blue. I worried a tree is not all we were going to kill on this trip.

"You can only buy marked trees. Prices are on the tag. Just chop it down and drag it back here to the main aisle. I'll mosey on back and pick ya up," yelled the homeowner/tractor driver as he puttered away.

I turned to my left and flipped over a tag on a tree shorter than me. Seventy-five dollars! At least we wouldn't have to worry about marks on our ceiling this year. These prices made no sense. I was chopping it down, and I was dragging it around, and I would pay more? I scratched my temple and did the married-guy-with-kids math. Yep, checked out. I exhaled and started walking down the row.

I was only near The Better Half and the girls for a moment before my fat goldendoodle started dragging me in the opposite direction. I jerked on the leash, but it was pointless. All of a sudden, she squatted and dropped a steaming turd. I reached in the back pocket of my jeans and pulled out a plastic bag. Now I got to carry a bag of warm poop while picking out an overpriced tree that we had to harvest ourselves. I looked down at my dog, and I swore she was laughing at me.

"Laugh it up, furball," I whispered. "I might have forgotten Kate's coat, but I remembered two plastic bags for you. Poopasaurus."

We wandered back to the family.

"I don't think our tree is in this area," said The Better Half as she carefully inspected two trees that were exactly the same.

"Yeah, let's go to the much cheaper area."

She chuckled while we stood in the main aisle and waited for the tractor to come again. Claire, the four-year-old, started doing jumping jacks to try to stay warm. I coached her on how to put her thumb out like a hitchhiker. I would have done it myself, but I had a dog leash in one hand and a steamy bag of poop in the other. The Better Half was rubbing Kate's hands, trying to keep her blood flowing. I felt like we were on a survival show.

The tractor sputtered to a stop next to us. We all climbed in the hay wagon. It was full of excited moms and cold kids. And depressed dads. The tractor cut deep ruts into the mud as it inched us to the other side of the yard.

As soon as my feet hit the ground, the dog pulled me in the opposite direction of my family. And pooped again. Now I was holding two bags of poop. I started looking for my family by peering over the overpriced trees. I thought I saw them at the end of the next row. As I was walking, I saw two figures tucked between Douglas firs on my left. A visibly pregnant lady and her husband were screaming at each other. Just screaming. She broke into tears. This place was hell. Seriously.

"This is the one!" yelled The Better Half as I approached.

"It is perfect. Looks exactly like all the rest," I replied.

She shoved the saw toward me, but I deflected it and grabbed Kate, who snuggled into my lumberjack shirt. The Better Half got down on all fours and went to sawing. This bow saw was much more efficient than the one I had used. I yelled "timber" as our overpriced tiny tree fluttered to the ground.

"Abby, heel," I said to my goldendoodle as I dropped her leash so I'd have a free hand to help The Better Half carry the tree to the main aisle. Abby took off in the opposite direction. I got the tree to the pick-up spot, handed off Kate, and ran in the direction of Abby.

There was a small retaining pond in the corner of the lot. It had two ducks in it. Abby decided she was going to catch those ducks despite her owner, dressed like Paul Bunyan and running across the tree farm, screaming at her to stop. The ducks started to quack as Abby barreled into the pond. Their quacks sounded a lot like laughter as they easily evaded the clumsy goldendoodle swimming in circles. Abby gave up, exited, shaked, and sprinted away from me.

She finally stopped in front of a beautiful Frasier fir. She sat as I approached. Then I realized she was not sitting; she was pooping. Again. I hadn't brought three plastic bags. I grabbed her leash, and we both ran. I would like to apologize to the people who undoubtedly paused to admire the Frasier fir in aisle two and stepped in steamy dog poop.

A white miniature poodle sprinted right in front of us. Abby lunged after her, but I was able to wrestle her back. An elderly Asian man in a fedora appeared out of nowhere. He was winded and grabbed his knees before talking to me.

"You have bag?" he asked in broken English.

"No. I used them all."

"Dog poop THREE times!" he stated before disappearing into the forest of Christmas trees in search of his white dog.

Back at the plywood shack, my kids munched on sugar cookies while I begrudgingly handed over my credit card to the chubby lady who undoubtedly owned the place and was married to the guy on the tractor. A property paid for with overpriced Christmas trees. I was a little ticked. Why hadn't I thought of this? I started wondering how many Christmas trees my yard could hold. After the girls finished their cookies and color started to come back in their lips, The Better Half decided on the division of labor.

"How about I take the girls and dog to the car while you get the tree?" she asked. This was the famous question that was really an order. Things had already been decided. I shrugged and stepped outside the shack holding a numbered tag, so I could make sure no one stole my tree. Since they all looked the same.

Two big guys in their twenties came up, dressed just like me. Two more Paul Bunyans. They looked like twins and reminded me of Darryl and Darryl from the old TV show *Newhart*. One of them asked if I wanted a "fresh cut." I refrained from interjecting profanity into my positive reply of "Yeah."

My tree got a fresh cut, and again, it was shoved into a fishnet stocking. All ready to be crucified in our living room for a month. Darryl smiled and handed me a small spool of baler twine.

"Will you guys help me get this tied on top of my SUV?" I asked.

"Naw, we ain't that type of operation," he answered with a chuckle.

They were a "you park in the mud, you chop it down out of our yard, while Dad drives a beat-up tractor around, and mom sits in a plywood shack eating sugar cookies, while we shove overpriced trees into fishnet stockings all day" kind of operation.

Darryl pushed the freshly cut stump in my hand with a grin. I smiled and bent down with the intention of tossing this tree on my shoulder. My smile faded as my back failed. Even small trees are surprisingly heavy. I looked across a football field expanse toward my SUV. I could see steam coming from my exhaust. I knew my family was toasty warm and listening to Christmas carols on the channel that starts Christmas music the day after Halloween. I should have gotten The Better Half to come help me, but I decided to solve this problem like a man. In the dumbest way possible.

I dragged that tree through the stinking mud all the way to my car. By the time I got there, it was two toned. I stood next to my SUV and squatted down to hoist it up on top. I got close. Close. Its needles painted the back window of my vehicle in mud as it slumped back to the ground.

"Hey buddy, looks like you could use a hand," said my old college roommate, Jeff, as he stuck his head out from behind the back of the vehicle. I hadn't seen him in months. I gave him a big lumberjack hug.

"You getting a tree?" I asked.

"Naw, they're too short and expensive here. I just bring the family here for the experience and the free sugar cookies. I'm actually headed to the Walmart parking lot right now to get my tree."

He was so smart. Here was a guy who learned something in college. I was the dummy paying for his sugar cookies.

We both crouched and hoisted my tree onto the roof rack like it was a scrawny, overpriced six footer. Which it was. Jeff grabbed the baler twine out of my hand and got to tying the tree. He tied it in about thirty different places. Good strong knots. He jerked on the trunk to make sure everything was secure. I suddenly recalled something about Jeff; he feigns like he knows something, even when he doesn't.

"You ever tie a tree to a roof rack before?"

"That's not going anywhere," he answered, as every male in the history of time was required to answer when tying something down.

"I know. How do I get it off?"

I pictured driving around in July with the skeleton of a Christmas tree still tied to my car. In a fishnet stocking. It dangling off the front like a hunter's buck.

"Been real, bro. Gotta get to the Walmart lot before all the fifty-dollar trees are gone."

I slid into the seat of my toasty car. Christmas carols played over the radio. Kids laughed in the back seat. The Better Half gave me a big hug and kiss on the cheek.

"See, that wasn't so bad," she whispered.

I just stared straight ahead in a catatonic trance, trying to repress everything that just happened. I finally responded as I shifted into reverse.

"I couldn't lift the tree to carry it across the parking lot. I had to drag it to the car. Half of it is covered in mud. Like totally covered."

She was quiet for a good long while. I felt the need to fill the silence.

"I have a plan to fix it. Do you think Walmart sells power washers this time of year?"

The Better Half finally looked over at me. "In the fall, we are going to a pumpkin patch to get our pumpkins. And we may be going to an apple orchard, too. Don't forget to buckle up."

Buckle up. Buckle up, indeed.

Me: Claire, why do you have these feathers in this drawer? Where did you get these?

Claire: From that pillow. Every time I slam it on the ground, I can pull feathers out.

Me: That's because it is a feather pillow. Why are you keeping them in this drawer?

Claire: I'm gonna make a turkey. Gonna have a pet turkey in my room.

Tonight's dinner table conversation:

Claire: Dad, we need to work on our fake sneezes. Repeat after me, "AHHH-CHOO."

Me: Achoo

Claire: No. I'll break it up. Say, "AHHH," like at the doctor.

Me: Ahh.

Claire: Now, "CHOO," like a train.

Me: Choo.

Claire: We have a lot of work to do before you are fooling anyone with that.

As part of their Christmas decorations, a friend had lined their sidewalk with two-foot-tall candy cane lights.

Me: Did you just lick that lawn ornament?

Claire: They look so delicious.

Me: They are plastic. And outside. All the time.

Claire: But what if they were real? I couldn't take that chance. Those would be some huge candy canes.

———

Tonight, four-year-old Claire asked for a cup of milk with her dinner. Which she promptly spilled down her shirt, into her jeans, and soaked her underwear. This necessitated stripping in 9.7 seconds and eating naked. Baby Kate was laughing so hard she dumped her bowl of soup on her own head. And that was dinner.

———

Claire: Can I have something else with my waffle for breakfast?

Me: What do you want?

Claire: How about a bologna sandwich and a car?

Me: How about apple sauce?

Claire: Deal.

———

The Better Half had to work late. I gave the girls their bath and tried to get them ready for bed.

Me: Would you two please stop running around your room naked. You need to put on your PJs and settle down.

Claire: Listen, Dad, since we're a team, I'll tell ya, when you just get done living a WHOLE day, you're pretty happy. That's just the way it is.

Me: Good point. Continue until exhausted. Don't tell Mom.

———————

Claire: I think I see poopy floating in my goldfish tank.

Me: Probably. All animals poop.

Claire: We really need a pet that doesn't poop. What doesn't poop?

Me: Nothing. They all poop.

Claire: Elephants poop out their trunks. Did you know that?

Me: No, they do not. I hope they teach you something in that preschool we are paying for you to attend.

———————

In my teens, I worked at a toy store called Toys "R" Us. They only sold toys. They hired dozens of workers to move toys. I was one of them. Somehow, a four-year-old and a toddler moved the equivalent of a toy store from the playroom to the living room while I was turned toward the stove fixing dinner. It's like they are evil Keebler Elves. It's going to take The Better Half a long time to put all of this back.

The ratio of adult females to males at the local water park this afternoon: 132-1. I was the one. This would be the best summer ever if I were into soccer moms. But I'm not.

Dear Fisher-Price,

Thanks to the quality of your walkie-talkie toys, my five-year-old and I can talk between rooms. She can also hear the truckers talking on the highway. She learned some new words. Awesome.

Me: Claire! What have you and Kate been doing in this bathroom? It is covered with water! You even got water on the ceiling!
Claire: We were playing water buffalo. It's a new game I invented.
Me: Both of you get out. I have to clean this up. I swear, you two are going to drive me to drink.
Claire: If you need a drink, I know where there is a whole bunch of water.

Tonight, three-year-old Kate decided to do her bedtime prayer in the form of an interpretive dance. We will either be very blessed or get a lot of rain.

Claire and Kate walk up from the basement without any shirts on.
Me: Why aren't you wearing shirts? Quit taking your clothes off.
Claire: We were downstairs feeding our dolls. We just came up for a break.

Me: Let's try to keep our clothes on. Okay?

Claire: Dad, you don't know anything about feeding babies from boobies, do you?

Me: No. No, I do not.

Most guys get ready for the college men's basketball Final Four by eating wings and drinking beer; maybe some fries drenched in cheese and bacon also are present. Since I am stuck in a house of all females, we have a tea party. I just ate my lunch of uncrusted sandwiches off fine china and sipped milk from a tea cup. With my pinky finger held high. Seriously.

Steps to being a preschooler at our house:

    1. Find a container full of items like Legos, or blocks, or a plastic tea set.

    2. Dump.

    3. Walk away.

Claire: Would you still love Mom if she was black? Would she still be your wife?

Me: Yes. Without a doubt. I am so glad you brought this up. I would love your mom regardless of race. We hope to live in a society where people are judged by the content of their character and not the color of their skin. A famous man once said that. Our family believes that. So yes, if your mom was African American, she would still be my wife.

Claire: Okay. 'Cause on TV, there was a show with a black bear. And I wondered if Mom would still be your wife if she was a black bear.

Me: Oh. In that case, no.

Me: Let's talk about our day while we eat supper. Who will start?

Kate: Today, I had the hugest poop ever!

Me: Not the conversation I was looking for.

Claire: How big was it? Show me with your hands like Dad does when he catches a fish. Except don't lie.

Me: No potty talk at dinner.

Kate: I don't know how this big of a poop got in me. Must be some kind of magic.

Claire: I wonder if there is a magician that uses poops? I'd like to see that.

Me: Okay. Everyone quiet. Just chew. Silently.

Claire: Good job reading that story, Dad.

Me: Thanks.

Claire: I really like how you did those different voices.

Me: I try.

Claire: Now read it again. And add a song at the end. Keep the voices but put them in the song, too.

Me: You watch too many Disney movies. Go to sleep.

———————

Me: Why are your gloves in your backpack and in a Ziploc bag?

Claire: I was sitting on the toilet at school, and I realized I was still wearing my gloves from recess. I took them off and set them on the floor. Then I bumped them with my foot, and they slid into the next stall. Jenna picked them up. I asked her to pass them back. She thought I meant throw them back, like over the stall. So, I stood to catch one, and it went right in the toilet.

Me: Why are they both wet?

Claire: I almost caught the second one.

DAD VS. THE GROCERY STORE

Beautiful fall Saturday. Exactly 68 degrees. The sun is shining, and the trees have just turned to a blaze of orange. I turn from the window and open the fridge. I realize we are out of milk. The skies darken.

The Better Half is at a women's luncheon. Probably drinking milk, unaware of my dilemma. I glance down at my two cherubs as we play a rousing game of Candy Land. A game of pure chance, although that makes my losing eight times in a row hard to explain.

"We are headed to the grocery store," I say, which causes six-year-old Claire to go get a pencil and paper rather than her shoes.

"I'll start the list," she says.

I'm scared. I was hoping it skipped a generation. The list making. Her mom has it. Has it bad. I'm afraid poor Claire's genes have taken control.

"I got the list right here," I say while tapping my temple. Claire throws a sarcastic look my way. A look that I also received yesterday when I refused to use the timer on the stove, resulting in her eating burnt pizza for lunch. Or the look I receive routinely after she beats me in games of Memory.

Three-year-old Kate starts crying for no obvious reason. This is just a warm-up for the tantrums she plans to unleash at the store.

One cannot be expected to put on such a performance without a little stretching.

"Go get on your shoes while I get my coupons."

The six-year-old comes back in about ten seconds dressed like she is ready to go on an expedition to the South Pole. The three-year-old takes ten minutes and comes back wearing only a swim suit. Seriously. I throw sweatpants on her while Claire tells me the dangers of "hippothermia." It's October. Focus. We need milk.

I circle the grocery store parking lot looking for the spot that will ease my escape after we finish. Rookie parents just pull into any old spot. Not me. This place has enough handicapped spots for an amputee convention. I respect that. But I can't leave Admiral Byrd and Ms. Swimsuit unattended in their car seats while I traipse across the entire parking lot returning an empty cart. Plus, I know my girls. If they must ding something when they open their door, it's better to ding the cart return than someone else's car. So, a spot right next to the cart return is ideal. A lady pulls out of such a spot. Perfect!

I get everyone out. Each girl holds tightly to one of my hands. If we had another kid, I'd be out of hands, and one would get hit by a car. I'd have to decide who went without a hand. I only have two hands. I better only have two kids.

The little one gets plopped in the cart and starts screaming as soon as her tush hits the plastic. I attach her shopping cart seat belt.

I let the six-year-old know, "Keep a hand on the cart at all times but don't push or pull. I'm watching you."

Claire takes two fingers and points them at her eyes, then at mine, while saying, "I'm watching you." Then Kate takes her two index fingers, points them at her eyes and then at me. She throws a squint in for effect.

"You two aren't watching me! I'm watching you!" I huff.

They both laugh.

We get some day-old donuts and a case of hard cider. Staples. At the end of the first aisle is a white-haired lady. She is old enough to have celebrated the end of prohibition. She has Dixie cups of alcohol set up for a beer and wine tasting. Claire's hand leaves the cart to grab one, but I feel a disturbance in the force, and I smack her hand away before she can spill the whole table.

"Would you like to sample one of our new wines, sir?" asks the old lady while handing me a cup with a shaking hand.

I consider possible responses:

1. Madam, I'm driving. A shopping cart.

2. Communion? Sure.

3. Can I have one for the kids? They love wine.

I go with: "It's going to take a lot more than a Dixie cup to repress this trip."

Turning the corner, I pick up two cans of mushroom soup to compare them. Is this one of the products where the store brand tastes the same as the name brand or where the store brand tastes like crap? I place them both in the cart and look for a coupon. Kate turns and hiccup/pukes on both of them. Decision made. Buying both. I better find that coupon. And a recipe that uses mushroom soup.

As we turn into aisle four, Claire bumps a pyramid of spaghetti sauce jars, sending one to the tile floor, and it sounds like a gunshot. The spilled sauce resembles a murder scene. Why can't they stack cans like normal people? I get a discount if we dent one of those. No one is in the aisle, and I consider leaving everything, including my kids. Instead, I flag down an older employee, who uses a corded telephone sticking out of a pillar to summon a stock boy and a mop.

I apologize to the stock boy for the mess. He says it's no big deal, but his eyes betray him, and I can tell he hates us. I teach junior high. One day, he'll undoubtedly have a stinky, farty, smart aleck kid that I will be forced to educate. We're even.

Just as he finishes, the god-like voice of the old man comes over the store speakers and summons him to aisle six for another spill. He gives me a little scowl.

"Hey, we haven't even been to aisle six. That's not us."

We slowly work our way through the cereal aisle, the girls begging for every sugar-filled, cancer-causing, obesity-inducing food that just happens to be placed right at their eye level. That Trix rabbit could not be staring any harder. Cap'n Crunch's eyes seem to be following us like one of those haunted-house portraits.

I head down the paper towel/toilet paper aisle to get a break from the whining. On the top shelf, there are packages of toilet paper with like fifty rolls. The package claims they are triple rolls, and it will last for months. I remember being a single guy and wondering who bought these? Who could need that much toilet paper? I live with three girls. I get down the giant package and shove it under my cart. We'll be out in two weeks. And I still don't know where it all goes.

Next on the list is some kind of feminine product listed as "light days" on the white board on the fridge. I start scouring the maxi pad/tampon/who-knows-what aisle. There are a thousand boxes, but none that say, "light days."

"This is boring," says Claire.

"Well, you can read a little. Get on all fours and check that bottom row."

The stock boy foolishly wanders down our aisle and asks if we need help. Soon, there are three of us looking through box after box.

"Found it!" I yell like I just won the maxi pad lottery. Big box, too. I have no idea how long a box of these last. I wonder if they sell them like the toilet paper. I have a house full of girls. I picture a future of me pushing around a shopping cart with nothing but toilet paper and feminine hygiene products.

We finally make it to the checkout line. I breathe a deep sigh of relief and flip through *People* magazine to see which celebrities look horrible at the beach so I can feel better about my dad bod.

"I gonna poop," declares Kate.

"Can't you hold that boneless brown trout for five more minutes? Seven minutes. Give me seven, and I'll get us home."

"I feel it coming out."

Crap. Literally.

I leave my valued place in line and aim my cart toward the bathrooms. They seem a football field away. I picture ice cream dribbling down the sides of the cart, flies circling my carefully chosen, slightly expired, half-price pot roast.

"Pooping" is all I hear whispered. I start running while Claire is dutifully trying to follow the "keep one hand on the cart" rule. At this point, she is hopelessly flying behind, legs flailing. I get in front of the restroom and slam on the brakes, Fred Flintstone style. Claire flies right by.

Dilemma time.

Do I send them into the women's restroom alone? I'm not sure they are strong enough to ever get that door open again. Or do I bring a three-year-old and a six-year-old into the men's room? I figure I lose either way.

I push the door to the men's room open and glance in. Big, clean, and vacant. The little one grunts, and I decide to press our luck.

We all three get situated in the handicapped stall, and I say a little prayer that some poor chap doesn't roll in confined to a wheelchair. Kate settles in. She asks us to sing her a song. She grunts for a long time.

"I thought you were going in your pants?" I say.

"That was the baby one. It's already swimming. Now I got to push out this big daddy."

We stand in her stink cloud for what seems like forever.

"I thought we were a team. Me and you. This is not how you treat your teammate," says Claire while holding her nose. She is reading graffiti on the stall wall. She says that we should call Jenny at 867-5309. I laugh out loud.

Claire steps backwards, and the stall door bangs open. Right then, a store employee walks in, probably getting ready to enjoy the only respite in his day. Kate sees him in the mirror and starts screaming. We are two-thirds female, in a handicap stall, and some poor guy is getting screamed at for innocently walking into the men's restroom. He's also African American, which makes us look racist on top of everything else. Claire has her fingers in her ears. Kate suddenly stops screaming. I grab the stall door and slam it shut.

"All done," Kate whispers. "Wipe me."

"We are going to stay in here until that man leaves. You created quite a scene," I say. I look out through the crack in the stall door. Scared him off.

I get my defrosted cart of food rolling again toward the checkout. There is a chubby man with a white beard and glasses smiling as he works his register. Both girls go silent. Afraid to make eye contact. We've been through this before. They think he is Santa. His line is really long, and I move over one. The girls look relieved.

I pull in behind a lady wearing a pantsuit and high heels with a screaming toddler in her arms. Her cart consists of two cases of wine. And nothing else. Not bottles. Cases. She gives me a look of, "This just got real."

The lady in front of her has a cart of nothing but dog food. She is telling anyone who will listen that her dogs are her children. I bet her dogs didn't just take a poop in the men's restroom and offend men, the handicapped, and African Americans in the process. These carts need car horns to go with the seat belts. She finally looks up and moves forward.

My turn. I slide a case of hard cider on the conveyer belt. The twelve-year-old checkout girl gets on the corded telephone to call someone that is over 21 to push the button to sell me my alcohol. The whole line waits. Finally, the same manager who just pushed the button for the wino in front of me wanders back over.

I grunt as I lug the case of alcohol back to my cart. Right then, Kate lets out a bloodcurdling scream like a pterodactyl being bitten by a T-rex. Ten lines of shoppers fall silent and stare at us. Her screaming. Me holding a case of alcohol.

"That ... is why I need this," I say to the store. They accept this, and everyone goes back about their business.

"With coupons and store savings, you saved $61.42," says the checkout girl as she hands me the receipt, "and you get another ten cents off gas."

"Thank you," I answer. But what I am thinking is: Glad I saved $61.42 because my six-year-old has a birthday party tomorrow at Build-a-Bear Workshop in the mall. Someone else's birthday party, mind you. Someone who will make me feel obligated to spend my $61.42 on a Kisses for You Kitty doll, dressed in a Rapunzel dress. A cat doll. I hate cats.

Instead, I smile and push my way out the automatic doors.

I get everyone buckled in and groceries packed into the trunk. I drive home. Finally, I pull into the garage and turn off the car. Exhale. I hear sweet Claire, my teammate, whisper from the back seat, "Weren't we supposed to get milk?"

Claire: Dad, a slumber party is the best. You get to spend the night with your best friend. You and Mom get to have a slumber party every night!

Me: I'm afraid there is not much slumber anymore. And no party.

Claire: What happened to your slumber party?

Me: You. And then your sister. Party's over.

Me: Did you forget to flush last time you were in this bathroom?

Claire: No, I didn't. I was saving that to show you. Biggest. Poop. Ever.

Me: Thanks.

Conversation at Grandma's House:

Me: Hey, I'm going downstairs to take a shower. In about five minutes, come down and bang on the door, wiggle the door handle, and try to talk to me.

Claire: Why?

Me: It's just really hard for me to shower unless someone is doing that.

Dear Claire,

It is called ChapStick, not LipStick. I'm going to have to insist you use the proper name. Let me give you an example of you using the wrong name. Tonight at church, you yelled, "Dad, do you need to put on some lipstick? You put it on all the time at home." This caused two elderly ladies to look hard at my lips.

Thank You,

Dad

At the trampoline park today. I am the only guy, and there are like fifty moms here. This lady strolls in, pays her money, and sends her two kids off to jump. She sits across from me and sets an alarm on her phone. And goes right to sleep. Doesn't move for an entire hour. Her alarm goes off; she gets her kids and walks out.

I am so mad. Why haven't I been doing this? A twenty-dollar nap! This lady is a genius.

Bedside Conversation:

Kate: I smell chocolate. Come closer. Let me smell your breff.

Me: I am here to give you one last sip of water and say good night.

Kate: Did you eat chocolate cake? Let me smell your breff.

Me: I'm going to get you a glass of water. Don't concern yourself with what I do downstairs after your bedtime to compensate for the stress you cause.

Kate: I'll have a drink of water. And a piece of chocolate cake to go with it.

Claire has gotten caught up in the Chuck E. Cheese false economy. She has a stack of tickets from playing games there. She feels these have great value, despite the fact they would not buy a kazoo in the actual Chuck E. Cheese. She tried to give her grandpa five tickets to cover his bill at the grocery store. She offered me ten tickets to pay for a Disney vacation. I told her it would cost six million tickets. She said she might have that many; she would have to count again. Pretty sure we do not have a future accountant on our hands.

The restaurant we ate at tonight had a table right next to the women's restroom. Kate used the restroom, then stopped at that table to tell the young couple eating there all about it: "Sorry I took so long in there. I had to poop. It was a big splasher."

Claire: Hey Dad, I heard boys have something between their legs called a peanut. Is that right?

Me: You know our thirty-ninth president was a former peanut farmer. And he taught Sunday School at his local Baptist Church.

Claire: Wait, what?

Me: Good talk. If you have any more peanut questions, ask Mom.

Dear Mom Who Tried to Sneak Her Kid into Swim Class,

    It was a great plan. Take your son swimming at the public pool. Have him mimic the students in the class and then slowly join in. Unfortunately, the teacher can count.

                                Thanks for the amusement,

                                  A Paying Parent

Car Seat Conversation

Me: I've had a long day, so no screeching on the ride home.

Claire: I just want to say I'm a big fan.

Me: Of what?

Claire: Of you, Dad. I'm your biggest fan. I'm so glad we are a team.

Me: I was having a bad day. Until now.

I got a horrible ear infection. I went to the doctor, and I had to bring both girls with me. In the exam room, Kate is screaming in my face while Claire is using the doctor's stool as a Sit 'n Spin. The nurse comes in and asks me a battery of questions.

Nurse: Would you say you drink alcohol: Never, Rarely, Sometimes, or Frequently?

Me: Before I had kids, it was rarely. Now? What was the last option again?

Today, being Saturday, I was woken up at 6 a.m. by two little girls jumping on my stomach. I pushed both of them to the other side of the bed. Then I hear the little one whisper: "If we kick him hard together, I bet he'll roll right off the bed."

Time to put Claire to bed and read from our never-ending book series: *Little House on the Prairie*. This series contains books like *Little House in the Big Woods*, *On the Banks of Plum Creek*, and *By the*

Shores of Silver Lake. I call it: Why Pa Can't Seem to Hold a Job or Stay in One Place.

———————

Me: You need to eat four more bites of your dinner.

Kate: I can't. Make me a deal, pleeeeease.

Me: Okay, just this once. Two more bites of pork, two more bites of peas, and one bite of sweet potato.

Kate: That's why I love you, Daddy. You always make special deals for me.

Me: Yeah. Don't ever learn math.

———————

Kate: Are you excited about Pearl coming tomorrow? You know, Grandpa Pearl.

Me: His name is Burl. Grandpa Burl.

Kate: Well, that's no fun.

Me: You're right. He has white hair. Most importantly, he has two hearing aids. You can call him Pearl. He'll never know.

Kate: Yeah. Pearl is a lot prettier.

———————

Kate (crying): What did Claire just whisper to you? I'm so mad.

Me: Why are you upset?

Kate: I can't take people having secrets. She's probably whispering something about me!

Me: She didn't say anything about you. Now, tell me why you are upset.

Kate: I'll whisper it in your ear.

Me: I brought you to the library for a reason. Get a book. Sit down. And silently read.

Kate: I can't read. I'm four years old.

Me: I don't care. Pretend.

I made the girls root beer floats for dessert. Just like the ones I loved as a kid. They went over like a fart in church.

Claire: It's burning my tongue.

Me: No, it is not.

Kate: Super spicy! Yuck!

Me: You two have just ruined your own childhoods. Go get jobs and move out.

Pulling the car into the garage, I hear the four-year-old call out from behind.

Me: "Please stay buckled until the ride comes to a complete stop."

I overhear Kate talking on her play telephone.

Kate: Hello, police? We have a dad drinking way too much coffee over here. Better send someone out to stop him.

Me: Coffee is just the start. It's the weekend, kid.

———————

Claire: Dad, look at this puddle in our driveway. I think we have a real mystery on our hands. I'm going to have to investigate.

Me: It rained. Solved.

Claire: I believe a snow man died here. And now he is gone.

Me: Just like my sanity.

———————

Kate: I'm mad! But Daniel Tiger says, "When you're so mad that you want to roar, take a breath and count to four."

Me: With your temper, you might have to count to 100.

Kate: I can't count to 100 yet. Guess someone is getting punched.

———————

My girls go to a very diverse school.

Claire: Do you have a tall African American boy in your class?

Kate: They are all Americans.

Me: Amen, sister.

———————

Snow Day Conversation:

Me: No, you cannot have a candy bar as part of your lunch. It's not even noon.

Kate: But you already have a daddy drink.

Me: Is Snickers okay?

———————

Claire is sick and on the couch. Kate is jabbing her with items from her doctor play set.

Me: If someone has the flu, that's not a time for you to play doctor.

Kate: Sir, please go back to the waiting room. Let the professionals deal with this.

———————

Take our little girls ice skating? Brilliant idea. We had a bloody nose, bruised shoulder, and crying. And that was before we even left the house.

———————

Car Seat Conversation

Claire: Dad, you need to slow down.

Me: I'm not going fast. I'm going thirty.

Claire: You know, when you really think about it, thirty is a big number. Why don't you go a different number? Like four.

———————

Me: Okay, we need to get baths and get to bed. I'm not letting you play any more games.

Claire: You know one time someone else wasn't allowed to play in any games. And it was mean. You know who it was?

Me: Don't say Rudolph.

Claire: Rudolph.

———————

Me: Why do you keep standing next to me and pulling up my shirt? Why are you holding a pencil?

Claire: I'm marking how tall I am on you.

Me: I'm not your measuring stick. Plus, it will just wash off in the shower.

Claire: Hmmmm. …Where is a permanent marker?

———————

The night before Easter, I walk downstairs, and the girls have set up an elaborate "trap" with jump ropes, Legos, blocks, stuffed animals, and a magic wand. The middle is baited with Reese's Peanut Butter Cups.

Claire: Easter Bunny trap is all set! Think we will catch him tonight?

Me: I feel pretty confident that he's going to eat that candy. Probably while drinking bourbon.

Claire: Huh?

Me: Kate, hurry up! Get in the car! I need to get to work.

Kate: I need a necklace and sunglasses.

Me: What? Why?

Kate: A girl does not go out without her bling.

Me: Why do you want all black pajamas for your birthday?

Claire: So I can visit Japan one day.

Me: You think everyone in Japan is wearing black pajamas?

Claire: Duh, Dad. They're ninjas.

Kate: Every time you take me swimming at the rec center, we pass these machines you can work out on. You ever think of using those machines? You know, lose the gut.

Me: No.

Kate: If your belly gets big enough, you'll have to deliver presents to kids all around the world.

Me: Except one kid. Pretty sure she is on the naughty list.

Putting some time in behind the wheel of the Barbie Pop-Up Camper. I am Ken, as always.

Kate: You should have Ken kiss Stacy.

Me: Isn't he married to Barbie?

Kate: Yeah, but things are getting boring. Time to add some drama.

Me: Why are you two so interested in our puppy losing her teeth?

Claire: We are finding them and keeping them. We have six already.

Me: What? Why?

Claire: We are going to put them under our pillows one night. Trick the tooth fairy.

Kate: Yeah, we're going to be rich!

All day, Claire has been addressing me as: "Hi, best friend. We are a team. Me and you."

Amazing how that can make a person feel better.

DAD VS. THE HAIR SALON

It is near the end of an exhaustive day. I am a boxing referee. After every round of the girls' fighting, I send them to separate rooms instead of separate corners. I stare at the timer on the microwave, ticking away. They have one more minute until they can come out of their respective corners. And the little one is going to come out swinging. I pray for the sound of the garage door going up. The Better Half coming home to relieve me. That will be the bell that signals the end of today's fights. Fights in which this referee is the real loser. I will retire to the basement with a bottle of bourbon to lick my wounds.

The phone rings. It should be The Better Half saying she is one minute out. I reluctantly answer.

"Something came up at work," she says.

"Wait! What? You are still at work? Something came up at home too. Your daughters are trying to kill each other. Preschooler on preschooler violence is a rising problem in this household."

"Have you checked the calendar?" she asks.

"No, I have not. I'm too busy keeping your youngest daughter from committing murder."

I glance over at the calendar stuck to the fridge. There could not be more writing on this thing. All kinds of arrows pointing all over the place. It's like Einstein's blackboard. Then I see it. I feel the background pull away as in a movie when the main character sees something horrifying. It says, "Girls Haircut with Trudy at 5:30." It is 5:10, and it takes twenty minutes to get there. The Better Half quickly tries to apologize into the silence of the phone. I just hang up.

I wrangle the girls into the car and start driving. Trees zip past and I can see Claire in the rearview mirror. She is straining to see my speedometer.

"Hey, slow down! That sign said 35 and you are going 40!" she yells.

"That's just a guideline. I'm doing 70 in kilometers. Live a little," I reply. I can't blame her. She's got a little too much of her mom's rule-following in her.

I screech into a parking spot at a strip mall complex. Both girls start screaming at each other. I have never smoked. But I'd love a piece of Nicorette gum right now. I scream "ENOUGH!" into the back seat, which buys me a ten-second armistice to tell them to get out of the car without slamming the door into the car next to us.

The hair salon is an enigma to me. I only know barber shops full of old men, cutting the hair of older men, who don't have much left to cut. This is a portal where The Better Half goes after lunch and returns as I'm setting dinner on the table. She comes back with slightly smaller hair and a big credit card charge. The Better Half considers this Trudy her close friend. Why? I am headed into the belly of the beast to find out.

I walk in with a daughter on each side. One in each hand, holding them apart like they are pit bulls ready to fight. There are partitioned booths on either side of me. I walk past half a dozen booths to a central desk. Behind the main desk is a kitchenette and what appears to be a Lowe's paint center. Interesting.

I quickly glance around like a Navy Seal in a terrorist hideout. I got seven women and one effeminate male. I'm surrounded by estrogen on every side. My little one picked a fine time to forget her plastic lightsaber. I might need backup. The cantina scene in *Star Wars* is feeling vaguely familiar right now.

The stylist to my left looks me up and down and then raises an eyebrow. I know she's thinking, "Your kind isn't welcome here." I glare at her. I've already done swim lessons with the soccer moms, story time at the library with all women, and yesterday I bought a value-size box of tampons. This ain't my first rodeo, lady.

She walks over to the center desk to tell me Trudy will be right with us. She motions to a pair of couches. The girls sprint over as I grab at them and get air. Either they are getting quicker, or I'm getting slower.

My daughters simultaneously grab magazines with nearly naked women on the cover. Why would a place that serves all women have girly magazines? Claire opens right to an article titled "Ten Ways to Snag a Man." I slap the magazine to the floor.

"You can read that after you get married. In thirty years," I say.

"I can't even read yet!"

"Doesn't matter."

Kate is staring at a pair of anorexic girls in bikini bottoms holding up bananas. I'm ruining her body image before she turns five. She's never going to eat again. And I was going to drive through McDonald's on the way home.

I grab the magazines and lay them face down on the coffee table. Half-naked women are on the back covers. Why are they trying to sell clothing with naked people? Why can't everyone just read fishing magazines like at my barber shop? "Ten Ways to Snag a Bass" seems much more appropriate. No one is getting body image issues from fat bald guys holding up trout.

I hand them my phone to keep them occupied and pick up one of the magazines. I do wonder how one would snag a man. The girls open a game on my phone where, ironically, they give a cartoon cat a haircut. When they are done, it automatically saves the picture on my phone. Now when anyone asks to see pictures of my girls, all I have are thirty pictures of a cat with a mohawk.

Trudy comes over and welcomes us. She gives each of the girls a hug. Trudy is in her late forties. She is wearing a white button-up dress shirt, leggings, and sparkly ballerina flats. She smiles and could not be nicer. She grabs Kate's hair and pulls it up.

"How do you want this cut today?" she asks.

"Shorter."

"What about layering?" she asks.

"Sure."

"And what should I do about this double crown she has going on here?"

"Better leave one crown. She wants to be a princess."

"You have no idea what you want done today, do you?"

"None whatsoever," I answer.

Where I get my hair cut, there are no questions. Just a metal chair with hydraulics and the sound of buzzing clippers. Trudy giggles at my cluelessness. I smile.

"I can cut your hair, too, if you would like," she says.

"How much?"

"Thirty-five."

"Dollars?"

We both smile politely. It takes ten minutes to cut my hair. If that. I do some quick math. This lady could be making $175 an hour. I use my limited math skills again while glancing at my daughters. She better be able to cut their hair in 7.5 minutes. Combined.

Kate climbs up in the chair, and Trudy sprays something into her hair. Better be gold spritzer for what I'm paying. Claire spots a broom and dustpan and starts sweeping up the stall. Because that makes total sense: overpay for a haircut and do the person's work while you're there. Claire has inherited some terrible cleanliness genes from her mother. I was hoping it would skip a generation. She has to clean and organize everything. I decide to go back to the couch and find out how one can snag a man.

I sit next to two women tapping on phones with their pointer fingers, their hair covered in thin strips of tin foil. I'm sure it would stop the aliens from stealing their thoughts, if they had any. They are oblivious to my presence.

Behind them are two old ladies, each with a black purse that could easily hold a bowling ball. Each getting her hair died a different shade of blue. I wager there is at least a grand in cash in each purse. A Brink's truck carries bags with less cash.

Directly in front of me, a lady in her forties has a large tan satchel on her lap that wiggles every once in a while. I'm willing to bet there is a little dog in there. Or a baby.

I see her hairdresser using scissors to snip all around her head while not actually cutting any hair. The bag lady in the chair is just jabbering on, while the hairdresser interjects an "uh-huh" every twenty seconds. A dozen years of schooling to be a psychoanalyst or a year of cosmetology school. Same job.

I see a lady who is getting the exact same haircut that I have. High and tight. At three times the cost. I so want to tell her about my barber, Mike. He even uses a straight razor to shave your neck.

Behind me, I overhear a conversation of a lady getting a haircut for her son's upcoming wedding. Her soon-to-be daughter-in-law is standing next to her repeating, "Looks great, Susan," over and over. I glance back, and Susan shoots me an, "I can't believe he chose her" look. I wonder how her son got snagged.

Trudy brings Claire over by me and washes her hair in a special sink that has a half-circle cutout in the front. Then she puts Kate's head under a dryer that covers seventy-five percent of her head. She looks like an astronaut. But she's smiling. Claire gets her hair braided. I wonder if I am paying extra for all this.

Five minutes later, both girls come up to me with smiles. Their hair looks the same, but now it's braided. I'm counting the hair washing as the bath for today.

At the counter, Trudy smiles and says, "twenty-five." I'm tempted to hand her two quarters and tell her to keep the change, but I refrain. I hand over my credit card. The receipt has a place for a tip. I tip a person that makes over a hundred dollars an hour? My barber deals in cash only, and the tip he gets is that the fish are biting on white jigs this time of year. I begrudgingly write down a five on the line. I'm buying that vacuum/hair cutting system when we get home. Trudy hands each girl a piece of candy as we walk out.

I get both girls buckled into the back seat, and they yell in unison, "We're hungry!" while suckers are falling out of their mouths. I tell them that I am going to buy a really fast car with the college funds I've been amassing. They are both going to cosmetology school. Their mom is a corporate lawyer, and she doesn't get $100 per hour. Plus tips.

I drive through McDonald's wishing they sold bourbon. The Better Half calls.

"Meeting got out early. I've been at home for a while. Kind of bored," she says.

"Well, I've had fun. I did read an interesting article in *Cosmo* about how to snag a man."

"Oh yeah. How would I snag a man like you?" she asks with a laugh.

"Stop getting $100 haircuts."

———

Me: The dentist said to use a pea-sized amount of toothpaste.

Kate: I'm more of a string-bean person.

Me: I'll adjust the toothpaste budget accordingly.

Claire: Would you be mad if someone peed a little in your closet?

Me: What horrible choices have I made in my life to get to this point?

Claire: It started when you told us to get ready for a bath, and we started a game of naked tag.

We took the girls to play laser tag. A man stood in front of all of us and explained the rules. Kate somehow took those directions as: "just follow your dad around and shoot him in the back one thousand times." Because that is all she did.

Me: You two kids have stressed me out enough today. I'm going upstairs to take a hot shower.

Kate: How hot?

Me: The sun.

Kate: I just love you so much.

Me: I love you too!

Kate: Well, this is awkward.

Me: Why?

Kate: I was talking to this piece of bacon.

Our first stop after entering the zoo is the flamingo exhibit. Two flamingos immediately start having an "afternoon delight" right in front of us.

Claire: We just get here, and we get to see a flamingo give another flamingo a piggyback ride! Best day ever!

Me: It's definitely starting with a bang.

The girls got me a Fitbit device for Father's Day. They also wear one. At dinner, we compare step counts.

Me: I'm at five thousand one seventeen.

Claire: I got seven thousand and ten.

Kate: One million. Exactly.

I read a parenting article that said I need to ask specific questions to get to know my kids.

Me: What was the number one best thing that happened at soccer camp today?

Claire: A boy got kicked right in the balls.

Me: Now I know you better. Thanks.

Parent fail #437

Last night, the Tooth Fairy gave the money to the wrong kid.

Me: First grade is too early for a boyfriend.

Kate: I don't have a boyfriend.

Me: Good.

Kate: I have like twenty.

Claire: I believe in Santa.

Me: Good for you.

Kate: Not me. I'm bad all year except right at the end. And I still get presents. He's either fake or dumb.

Everyone has New Year's resolutions of losing weight, exercising, and saving money.

And I'm here just trying to get my ponytail game strong.

9:06 p.m.: Kate lost her front tooth. We all cheer for her.

9:07: The Better Half realizes that neither of us has any cash.

9:08: Consider putting family heirloom under her pillow.

9:09: Make stiff drink.

9:10: Decide to steal her allowance and then give it back to her as the Tooth Fairy.

———————

Kate: When you were young, did you think you'd get married and have kids?

Me: Married? Yes. Kids? Yes. A kid like you? No one could see that coming.

———————

My first grader wanted me to take her to the school "Spring Fling" dance. She promised:

    A. Lots of dads are coming

    B. I wouldn't miss any sports on TV.

    C. Everyone will be dressed up.

These were all lies. All. Lies.

———————

Me: I can't give you a piggyback ride. It will hurt my back. Some dads have kids when they are young. Then there is your dad.

Kate: Awwww ... instead of a Daddy, I got a Saddy.

———————

I was having a tough day. The girls started spontaneously clapping in the car.

Claire: Let's give it up for Dad! He's my teammate! He drives us home from church and makes us Sloppy Joes for dinner!

Kate: Best dad ever! We love him!

And old dad's heart grew three sizes that day.

Kate: Hey Claire, chew with your mouth closed like a princess instead of like a cow.

Me: You may go to time-out on the stairs for being rude.

One minute later:

Kate: Hey Claire, I'm down the hall on the stairs, AND I CAN STILL HEAR YOU CHEWING!

Last night, while I was on the couch watching basketball, Kate starts crying upstairs and screaming, "Daaaaadddy!" Finally, there is a time-out, and I wander upstairs. Kate informs me that she had to wash with Dove soap. I fail to grasp the gravity of the situation. A sopping wet first grader informs me that Dove makes a person smell like "poop." And she doesn't want the last memory of her classmates, right before spring break, to be of Kate smelling like a turd. I let her know that neither I nor the makers of Dove soap were aware of this fecal smell. She accuses me of pandering due to shared DNA. I then pretend to be a bloodhound and sniff her arms. I assure her that she smells wonderful. She tacitly accepts this and proceeds to bed. This is not an atypical bedtime. And The Better Half wanted more kids.

———————

Spent the afternoon at the pool.

Claire: Dad, back in your day, the olden times, did they have swimming?

Me: No. I predate water.

———————

Claire: Dad, thanks for not working out all the time and getting all rocky. When I lay on you to watch TV, I like a more pillowy dad.

Me: I prefer the term bean-baggy dad.

———————

Took the girls fishing at a local pond, and Kate hooked a rather large bass.

Me: Today is very important. Second only to your birth. You caught your first bass. I will call you Tricky Fish today. You tricked that big fish into getting caught.

Claire: I caught a bigger one last year.

Kate: Be quiet, Little Sunfish. This is my day!

———————

Think you are good at games? Try playing hangman with kids that can't spell.

Kate got me on her version of Neosporin spelled "Nelasrone."

Whoever called my cell at 5:17, sorry I missed your call. I took the girls to the pool. Here's how our conversation would have gone had I answered:

"Hey, I'm in the family restroom at the pool while the little one poops. For an hour. I figured out she likes to poop when we go out because she can use all the toilet paper she wants. Which is true, because I'm not paying for it. Hey, any tips on getting a seven-year-old back into a wet swimsuit? Keep in mind that I currently do not have any butter on my person. Hello?"

The girls were fighting today. I took them to a Japanese noodle restaurant. I ordered each one a bowl of noodles and told the waitress that they only get chopsticks. They don't know how to use chopsticks. No more fighting.

Kate stayed home from school sick. I took her to the doctor, and then we had to go to the pharmacy to pick up her prescription. They now look up patient information using birthdays, leading to this conversation:

Pharmacy Tech: Patient date of birth?

Me: I forget. That's a question for her mom. Kate, when is your birthday?

Kate: November 6.

Me: We need the year, too. How old are you? I can work this thing out backwards.

Kate: With your math skills, I might be sick forever.

———

Letting your kids buy Christmas gifts for others is always an adventure. The 8-year-old tried to buy "Sex Kitten" lotion as a gift. For Grandma.

———

Claire: You have two bottles of daddy drink in the cart.

Me: Two bottles of bourbon. Two kids.

Claire: What if you had ten kids? Then what would you have?

Me: A keg.

———

Dear Camp Counselor,

    When my youngest gets there and immediately pukes, it's because she consumed ten thousand calories of sugar on the bus ride. She is not sick. We are not coming to pick her up. I don't even know where your camp is. Her mother and I are busy. All week.

        Thanks,

        Summer Dad

DAD VS. DISNEY

Before a wife and kids, I was a public school teacher renting a tiny room off some other single guy. I was coasting. No cares. I ate cereal for dinner. Lucky Charms, if I was indeed lucky. My worldly possessions could be stuffed into two black garbage bags and often were. I lived as a hermit crab, just backing into whatever shell felt comfortable.

The phone rang and reverberated off the pale walls of my tiny bedroom. It was my college friend, Kara. Kara was the best. No need for hello or other salutations.

"When is your spring break?"

"Month," I answered.

"You wanna go to Disney World? For like no money. You can bring your kid brother."

"Probably. Lemme check."

These were typical conversations among young single people. Long before The Better Half and her nightly diatribe and my screaming, relentless kids. Conversations were short and to the point. And had a point.

Kara went on to explain that she was the assistant band director at a small rural high school. The band was going to Disney to play in a parade. Disney charged the band a flat fee and gave them sixty student trips. For a band that has forty-five members. Even with chaperones, they had two trips left. Four hundred dollars would get us round trip bus fare to Florida, hotel, entrance to the Disney parks, food. Everything.

I told her I'd have to check with my brother and get back to her. I was unaware that a trip to the Magic Kingdom usually involved a second mortgage and the selling of a kidney. When I was a kid, we did not go on elaborate trips to Disney World. We went to see my grandma in Iowa. And stayed in a pop-up camper in her driveway. Five people in a tiny camper with no bathroom and no air conditioning. Why didn't we stay inside Grandma's two-story house? Because she was a hoarder. Whatever the Magic Kingdom entailed, it had to be better than that.

I called my brother, Josh.

"Is your spring break in a month. Exactly?" I asked.

"Nope."

"I got a trip to Disney for us. Cheap. I'll give you the money."

My brother did not seem super inclined to remain in school and gain knowledge. I called Kara back, and Josh and I were off to Disney.

I was a groomsman in a wedding in Western Michigan when the band bus left for Florida. I had to leave the wedding at midnight, drive back to Ohio, and catch a plane for Orlando, all without sleeping. I was young and single. Done.

Kara decided to drive her car down separate from the band. Josh and Kara picked me up at the Orlando airport, and we drove straight for Disney. I hadn't slept in a day and a half and had just crammed eighty inches of person into an airplane seat. The current me would die at the prospect of not sleeping and doing a full day at The Magic Kingdom. Me in my twenties? Oddly excited.

We pull up to the park, and the attendant looked down at our car while we fish for the six dollars to pay for parking. "Ohio plates? I'm from Ohio, too. It's free for you," she said while waving us in.

That's how we started our day. Free. My brother and I glanced at each other. This had the potential to be the greatest day of our lives. Although a pop-up camper in the driveway of a hoarder is hard to beat.

I was wearing jean shorts, a leather weave belt, a Nike basketball T-shirt, and basketball high tops. My brother was dressed almost exactly the same. I was ready for Mickey or a spontaneous game of pickup basketball.

Upon entering, the park is designed to make you walk through a version of Main Street USA. Photographers make you pose for pictures. I was a twenty-something. I wasn't buying any pictures of me and my dorky brother. Not when I had a perfectly good disposable Kodak camera in my pocket. We strolled through Main Street and headed to the right. A life-size Winnie the Pooh and Tigger appeared right next to me. I was just standing there, and a hundred people were lined up behind me. They were all clutching autograph books. I dug out my disposable camera.

"I smell something," I whispered to my brother with a sly grin.

"Like Pooh?" he answered.

I found out these character appearances were a big deal. No character could be in more than one place at a time in the park. No two Mickeys. And each autograph had to be distinct. And it could never change. A Mickey signature from 1970 had to be the same today. People make it their life goal to be these characters. And I was making fecal matter jokes. In front of a guy whose life goal was to dress up as Pooh.

Kara said she had to go find the band. She shoved several green slips of paper in my hand and said they were food vouchers. Josh and I took off on our amazing adventure.

We walked for no more than a minute when a beautiful girl appeared. She had black hair, dark eyes, and a tattered skirt. She was in her early twenties. I was in my early twenties. The Magic Kingdom had just become a little more magical. There was a grubby kid in front of me. She pushed him aside. Our eyes met. We were having a moment here.

I shoved my disposable Kodak camera in the hand of my brother as Esmerelda and I embraced. She smiled. I smiled. She had a male escort, who also tried to get into the picture. He was either feeling threatened by me, or his green tights were a little too snug. I elbowed him softly. His brow furrowed and eyes narrowed while Esmerelda and I giggled. I heard the click of my camera. She gave my hand a squeeze. I should have told her I was staying at a hotel about half an hour away, only accessible by bus. It's one of those thoughts you have in the middle of the night. I could have been with Esmerelda. I was much better looking than a hunchback.

We quickly realized that all the rides, with lines weaving back and forth like a mountain switchback, had an empty line titled "single rider." There were no singles at Disney. Just families with extended families and lots of strollers. We knew we could enter this single-rider line and run past everyone, since we were wearing basketball shoes. Jogging by, I failed to notice the screaming kids, dying dads, and sweaty grandparents minutes away from heat stroke. I was jogging through a war zone. It was like running on Omaha Beach on June 6, 1944, and not noticing anything.

When we got up to the ride, we could take any open single seat. Usually, we were right in front or behind each other. I recall jogging through the line for "It's a Small World," and it was just obscene. It started outside and coiled all over the place. Once you got inside, you were nowhere near getting on the ride. There were roped-off sections and bridges. Then you heard it, that incessant song.

A boat floated up, and I got in the front seat next to a family of three. The little girl next to me looked over with wide eyes, shocked to see someone alone. At Disney.

"Where is your family?" she asked.

"They drowned on Splash Mountain. But my ticket was only good for today. So ..."

She didn't talk again.

We hopped off and sprinted to ride the carousel. The line wound around the circular carousel like a vortex. We found another single-rider line. Empty. I jumped on a white stallion and laughed like a fool as the carousel went around and around.

At noon, we stopped by some tavern-themed food window. I ordered a cheeseburger meal and nervously handed the teenager behind the counter the wrinkled, sweaty, green food voucher. I was very hopeful she would take it because I only brought six dollars for the trip, and Disney food is not exactly a bargain.

"Thank you and have a great day," she said with a smile while handing me my food. Everything was in a cup. Even my cheeseburger. Weird.

Oh well. The takeaway was that Disney food is quick and free.

The rest of the day continued in the same manner. Skipping lines, paying for things with sweaty scraps of paper, and generally having a blast.

Near sunset we found Kara, and she mentioned that our park tickets were good for entrance to any of the parks. There were busses running everywhere, and as long as we were back in time to catch the band bus back to the hotel at midnight, we could do as we pleased. Josh and I gave each other a simultaneous wink and sprinted for the parking lot.

We hopped on a bus headed for Animal Kingdom. We were the only ones on the bus. Being young and dumb, I never questioned why. I did not know Animal Kingdom closed at dusk. Duh. The main attractions have to go to sleep.

I was under the impression that these parks would be right next to each other. This was not the case. By the time we were showing our tickets to get into Animal Kingdom, everyone was streaming out. The lady taking our tickets looked at us like we were crazy and stated that they closed in thirty minutes. She said we would have a hard time seeing "anything."

Josh and I looked at each other. Challenge accepted. I didn't run all those wind sprints in college for nothing. We would have to see "everything."

We ran for the middle of the park, and the plan was to branch out from there. I paused at The Tree of Life and marveled. It was this huge tree with all kinds of animals carved in it. A lady was putting a blue macaw in a cage.

"Hey, can I pet the parrot?"

"We're not supposed to let the guests touch the birds. But what the heck, we're closing for the night."

"What's the best thing here?" I asked while scratching the parrot's head.

"Safari ride. The line is usually hours long. But they are probably done for the day."

I bowed deeply, and we took off in a dead sprint toward a sign that said Safari. We were both yelling "we're coming" like idiots. We got to the entrance and sprinted through turnstiles and metal barriers. I nearly tripped as the ground was littered with pop bottles, puke, and pacifiers. I was too young to question what had happened here. I was running through the Cambodian Killing Fields of parenting without a clue.

A man in a safari hat waved us in. We jumped on the last ride of the day in the last two seats. It was tremendous. No one cared what we did. These workers were minutes from ending another day. The tour guide, tired of saying the same thing one thousand times, was cracking jokes. I leaned way out of my seat and slapped an endangered rhino right on the butt. It was a lot softer than one would expect.

We were the last ones to leave the park. A vendor was throwing away bags of unsold cotton candy. He handed us two bags. Totally free. Because that is Disney. Totally free. I ate a cotton candy as big as my head all the way back to The Magic Kingdom. Our bus driver was laughing his head off, saying over and over again, "Y'all crazy."

That night at The Magic Kingdom they had a parade. All these floats were covered with Christmas lights, and they played some incessantly cheerful music. People were literally dancing in the street. I was looking hard at every character dancing by.

"Looking for Esmerelda, lover boy?" my brother asked.

"Shut up. You looking for Pooh?"

They projected famous Disney movie scenes onto the giant Magic Castle, and a real live Tinkerbell flew across the park on a wire. The whole thing ended with fireworks.

That night, snuggled in my hotel bed, ready to get some sleep for the first time in two days, I looked up at the ceiling and thought, "This is the happiest place on Earth."

Fast forward a decade. I have now acquired The Better Half, and together, we have produced a six-year-old and three-year-old. And a minivan. And a mortgage. Your typical adult stuff. I'm still wearing jean shorts and basketball high-tops.

The Better Half remembers mentioning a want to go to Disney. I remember it more as, "We are going to Disney." I argued that maybe Disney would not be the best choice, as the three-year-old would only retain fleeting memories of the vacation, at best. Yet, my money would be permanently gone. We compromised by going to Disney.

I called a friend who was a Disney travel agent. She took our info, was very pleasant, and said she would call me right back with prices. Less than an hour later, the phone rang. I was standing in the kitchen. She said a number. It had to be equal to the band trip that I went on with my brother. Like the cost for the whole band. Then she added, "Of course, you'll have to add on airfare, transfers, and taxes and such." Of course. And I'll have to add a second mortgage onto my house.

I put my hand over the receiver and whispered one of those angry, on-the-phone whispers in the direction of The Better Half. She never even glanced up from the yogurt she was eating. I knew resistance was hopeless. I gulped hard and booked the trip. Spring break we'd go for broke.

The day before we left, The Better Half started with the list-making. She was going through reams of paper. Elaborate lists with sublists and little hand drawn boxes next to things, just begging to be checked. I had a gray duffel bag and no list. No worries, she had a list for me and a little suitcase. She checked a box as she handed it to me. I hoped going to the bathroom was on the list. I really had to pee, but like a kid on the first day of school, I was afraid to ask her permission. She instructed me to lay out everything on my list on my side of the bed and she would pack my suitcase. I did this without speaking.

My side of the bed was covered in stuff. I glanced at the tiny suitcase and headed for the bathroom. Without permission.

I strolled out, washed my hands, and looked at my side of the bed. Empty. There was no way. I checked under the bed. Nothing. It was like some kind of magic trick. I gingerly carried my tiny suitcase downstairs. This Jack-in-the-Box could have exploded at any moment. Jean shorts and basketball T-shirts everywhere.

The Better Half and I still hadn't spoken, and I had not made eye contact. It was tradition that we would have a big fight before every trip. Sometimes her detail-oriented personality drove me crazy, but then I realized, without it, I would probably be in jail. For instance, taxes are due on April 15, and by March 1 she usually has them done. I have no idea how the American system of taxation operates. I don't plan to learn.

I walked down the hall to check on six-year-old Claire and three-year-old Kate. Both had their own lists and were busy placing items all over their bed and waiting for the packing fairy to arrive. Claire had mesh shorts, T-shirts, athletic shoes, sweat bands. Kate had elaborate ball gowns with tiaras and a scepter. She was wearing fairy wings as she worked. The wings had a button on the back, and if you hit it, they would glow and make the sound of a harp being strummed. I stepped back into the hall and realized I was raising one Sporty Spice and one Posh Spice.

The next day was a blur of airplanes, van rides, and busses. At dusk, we arrived at Disney's Art of Animation hotel. I walked into the expansive lobby. A girl who couldn't have been more than twelve checked us in and pulled out a map. She told us to walk past Simba and friends, past Ursula, but if we hit Prince Eric, we'd gone too far. I wanted to die.

We walked past the dining hall and its wall of windows that looked over a pool of eight thousand kids trying to drown each other while a Disney movie played in the background on a giant screen. We walked. And walked. Soon I was carrying the girls' suitcases and my own. We got to a giant fiberglass statue of Simba from *The Lion King*. And pushed on. Trudging. Finally, we got to Ursula. She was the octopus-obese woman from *The Little Mermaid*. Seemed like all she was missing was a giant fiberglass Marlboro Red dangling from her lower lip. We wandered all over the place and finally found our room. Once, while backpacking Europe, I stayed in a youth hostel in Prague that used to be the Olympic village. It once housed all the athletes of the world. This hotel was bigger.

The room was small but clean. There was a plastic Ariel head glued to the wall and some stickers of a prince and some fish. Other than that, it was a cheap hotel room. That was not that cheap.

It had been an exhaustive day, so we settled in for bed. Got the girls into pajamas. The little one started using her bed as a trampoline. She insisted on sleeping with her parents. I let her know that she was a nutcase, as only her dad could. Eventually, everyone was nodding off except for the three-year-old. She was whispering to herself. At least it was in her own bed.

The Better Half woke up first. She had more lists and boxes to check. We needed magic bands, sunblock, sunglasses, and water bottles filled with ice from the ice machine down the hall. Check, check, check. Crazy, crazy, crazy.

As soon as The Better Half vacated the spot next to me, the little one appeared and snuggled up. I could hear her snoring. I got up to help The Better Half. Then Claire jumped out of bed, ready for the day. Our room was like a kicked ant's nest. Except for Kate, who looked dead. The Better Half looked up from her lists and yelled out some false consequence for not getting up. Kate was either getting abandoned at Little Mermaid Motel 6 or was going to be attacked by a giant Ursula. I put ice cubes on her feet as I was filling up the water bottles.

Finally, three of the four members of our family were standing at the door, sunglasses on, backpacks with water bottles dangling, smelling like Coppertone, while Kate snored.

Day one at The Magic Kingdom, and this was not the start we were hoping for. Time to poke the bear. The Better Half started dressing her while her eyes remain closed. She forced her limp spaghetti arms into a Mickey shirt and dumped her in my arms. I took two steps for the door, and she started screaming. She climbed down from my arms and calmly put on her sunglasses, upside down as usual, and slid on her Tinkerbell fairy wings.

We began the long walk to the cafeteria. It was attached to the entrance and across from the pool and nowhere near our room. And it was a beehive of crazy time. Picture your college or high school cafeteria. Now make everyone older, fatter, and add a couple kids to each person. Now put every single person in something Disney themed. Every. Person. I saw kids crying, moms screaming, and dads running around while sweating profusely. This was vacation.

I had the family tell me what they wanted, and I sent The Better Half to get seats, as there looked to be a real chance we would be eating on the floor. I grabbed a comically small brown tray and started carefully stacking breakable plates of food on it. I tightroped my way to the checkout line. The two families in front of me had some kind of meal plan. They touched their magic band bracelet to the metal Mickey statue, and he glowed green, and there was a pleasant little bell sound.

I walked up as some lady who looked like Alice from the Brady Bunch was furiously poking at a touch screen. I had orange juice, pancakes, an omelet, coffee, and oatmeal—the latter for The Better Half, who thinks she is eighty years old. I touched my magic band to Mickey. He glowed red and a big "Bong" rung out. The bald guy behind me faked coughs.

"You on a meal plan, honey?" asked Alice.

"I guess not," I answered while trying to balance my tray and fish my wallet out of my back pocket.

"Fifty-eight," said Alice.

"Fifty-eight?" I asked as though it might be cents instead of dollars.

She grabbed my credit card while I seriously considered punching the smiling Mickey statue in the face. I was tempted to ask if, like when buying expensive electronics, I could purchase some type of insurance in case I dropped this Jenga-stacked tray full of porcelain on the hard tile floor.

I walked to my family using little baby steps. Everyone gobbled down fifty-eight dollars of food in about fifty-eight seconds. Except The Better Half.

"Did you get the two sugar packets, like I asked?"

"Pretty sure they cost five dollars. Each. Eat up, Grandma."

Next, we took our backpack-toting, sweaty, water-bottle-swinging selves to the leper colony known as the Disney bus stop. This was where you got your first inkling that the hotel they took you to straight from the airport was nowhere near the beloved Magic Kingdom. It was just a fancied-up Motel 6 with stickers on the wall. You were actually in Georgia.

There was an entire little league baseball team at the bus stop. They were all wearing matching red and white uniforms. One little guy was even wearing a mitt. I was unsure what he thought he was going to catch around thousands of other people besides MRSA or Legionnaire's disease.

Next to the little all-stars was a gaggle of plus-sized women, all in ill-fitting pink T-shirts. Each shirt advertised natural oils. Some kind of hocus-pocus healing crap. Every shirt had the company name with Mickey ears on top. I realized that everyone at this bus stop was wearing something with Mickey ears. But me. I was wearing a T-shirt with a fish on it. I was very tempted to grab a marker and add ears to my rainbow trout. If plumbers had a retreat at Disney, they would have T-shirts with a plunger in Mickey ears.

Next to the bench that could not possibly accommodate all these people was a sign with illuminated numbers that told when the next bus would arrive. The numbers changed and bounce around at an alarming rate. Were we in *Back to the Future*? Was the bus a DeLorean? It said the bus would be here in eighteen minutes. Then eleven. Then nineteen. Had the bus backed up? Done another lap? This whole system seemed inefficient at best.

Finally, a city bus with Mickey ears rolled up and opened its doors in the front and in the rear. The entire baseball team piled in the front door, and I could see them running to the back of the bus to take up all the seats. A handicapped man in a red scooter, like the ones overweight people ride around on in Walmart, was patiently waiting at the back door. The driver got out and pushed a button next to the door. A ramp started to unfold at the slowest speed possible. I could hear metal grinding as it stopped then started again at a glacial pace. Its movement was accompanied by a loud beeping as though it might crush someone.

I had resigned myself to not getting on this bus, and I took a seat on the bench. The hocus-pocus oil ladies in the pink T-shirts were visibly impatient with the ramp and handicapped man blocking their access to the bus. And I was getting angry. Ladies, you sell oils and undoubtedly have some in your collective fanny packs. You have a machine running slowly. Add oil. That's what it was invented for. Or use your magic oil to heal the man in the scooter so he can just walk onto the bus. Or do both. Never again will you be in a situation where oil is literally the answer to all that is slowing you down. Show the world the magic of your elixirs. Instead, they huff and puff and toe tap until they can all waddle on the bus. Frankly, I was happy to see them go.

The bus disappeared toward central Florida. The "magic" Mickey sign, because everything here is magic, flashed that it would be twenty-five minutes until the next bus. I exhaled. Then it flashed one minute. I stood up and gathered the kids. Then it flashed twenty minutes. I sat back down and started looking in the surrounding bushes for some practical-joke-playing teenagers. Next, it flashed "arriving." I stayed seated but stretched my neck out a good deal. My daughters were playing tag in front of me, trying desperately to get hit by a bus or at least break a tooth on the concrete and ruin our day at the Magic Kingdom. Then there was a bus.

We got on, and there was a whole other set of oily ladies. This time, it was purple T-shirts with the aforementioned Mickey ears. They were distinct from the former bunch. I guess oils don't mix. These ladies were selling some kind of oil-candle device. I half-expected to be mobbed and sold candles by a dozen purple-shirted women and have committed to buying fifty dollars in candles before reaching the park. To be honest, the candles would have been cheaper than breakfast and a lot longer lasting.

The older lady next to me, with short white hair like a Q-tip, was droning on to another lady about how she needed to reach "diamond" level in the next few months. Then she could quit her job as a secretary and buy a condo on the beach. She just needed to recruit more people under her, because there were so few people above her. The temperature difference between the steamy outside and the air-conditioned bus made the windows accumulate condensation. I started outlining the shape of a pyramid on the window next to me. But the secretary was in too deep to notice.

Our bus rolled into the Magic Kingdom parking lot and got into a line of no less than fifty busses. Every bus took a turn pulling into numbered stalls like cows at milking time. Throngs of people of every race and creed spilled out and formed a rushing river of humanity streaming toward the park entrance. I picture some lost boy looking up like Simba during the wildebeest stampede in *The Lion King* and getting swept up, and the next thing he knows, he's at the foot of the Magic Castle. And his dad is gone.

From what I could see, every drop in this human river had one thing in common. Everyone was wearing Disney-branded everything. Except me. I became a little self-conscience of my fish shirt. There were matching Mickey bride and groom shirts, with a little veil for the bride supported by Minnie ears. Mickey ear hats. Goofy headgear. But Disney only lets it go so far. You are not allowed to actually dress like characters. Because people always take things to the extreme. One pasty white guy would show up in a sailor outfit with no pants claiming to be Donald Duck and ruin it for everyone.

We were swept toward the front gates where security guards checked everyone and everything. One security guard in a fluorescent yellow shirt was pointing at me. I'm tall; he was tall. We both probably played college ball. He knows a fellow baller when he sees one. Probably going to ask me if I can still dunk. I will not tell him I am too afraid to try because I would probably break my leg upon landing. I'll just say, "Maybe."

I got closer, and he reached out and gave me a fist bump.

"I could probably still ..." I say before he interrupts.

"Man, I do love to fish. That a rainbow trout on your shirt?"

"Maybe."

I realized this is probably the first non-Disney piece of clothing this poor man had seen in days, months, who knows, even years.

We entered the park, and there was a Mickey made of flowers. Next to that was a vendor cart overflowing with stuffed animals and other overpriced trinkets. The most offensive was a blue water bottle with plastic fan blades on the nozzle. With the obligatory Mickey sticker on the side. The vendor locked eyes with me while holding out the water sprayer, mister/fan combo.

"Only thirty dollars. Gonna be a hot one."

I was certain the look I gave him screamed, "Only a freaking moron would pay thirty dollars for that."

We were forced to pause in the middle of Main Street while a photographer took our picture with the Magic Castle in the background. To sell to us later. And we would probably buy it. The real magic in Disney was painlessly separating you from the contents of your wallet.

We strolled down old-timey Main Street. I half-expected men in bowler hats to bump into us and say, "Oops-a-daisy" or The Better Half to exclaim, "Oh fiddle-faddle."

The cobblestone street had turn-of-the-century shops like a candy store, ice cream parlor, and Starbucks. The Better Half stated that she wanted a coffee. I stuck my head into Starbucks. There were hundreds of parents in line, most of whom had not had their coffee. It was like sticking one's head in a hornet's nest. I noticed the prices were certainly not turn-of-the-century. I kind of hoped all the baristas would be Minnies and there would be a male Mickey manager with a handlebar mustache and a sign that said, "No Ducks Served."

I gave The Better Half a look that said, "The line for A Small World is shorter," and we all trudged on. We were no more than ten steps past Main Street and in front of the Magic Castle when it started.

"My legs are killing me. I can't go another step," exclaimed Kate while collapsing to the ground while Claire skipped around her in a circle.

"Use fairy power," I told her as I pushed the button between her shoulder blades, making her wings glow and causing a harp chime.

"Are you crazy? You can't use fairy power all the time. Like for this whole trip!" Kate replied, disgusted.

I hit the button again. Hoping those wings had five hundred magical reactions and they were on number four ninety-nine. Then I remembered that my list-making, crazy, Better Half probably had extra batteries on her person. Or I would have had to buy them in a Mickey Mouse-themed battery store. And they would cost twenty-nine dollars and have Mickey ears attached in some fashion. And somehow this would seem reasonable.

I carried Kate to the Dumbo ride because it was now after 10, and it was time for our first Fastpass. Basically, you got to cut in front of all the people in the normal line like the cool kid in elementary school. But you only got to cut three times a visit, and you had an assigned time to do it.

I walked up to our Fastpass line and tapped the bronze Mickey statue with my Magic Band, and Mickey glowed green, and a pleasant chime rang out.

"Couldn't do that at breakfast?" I whispered.

We took the old single-rider line I knew so well all the way to the front. A woman in lederhosen and a green pointy hat stabbed her hand in front of an effeminate potbellied man, the type that looked like he would try to walk a cat on a leash, as he was about to get on. She let me and Kate on instead. It was like we were the cool people cutting in the cafeteria line. The cafeteria in an insane asylum.

The ride was basically a fair ride with a fountain in the middle. Our fiberglass Dumbo elevated about 8 feet while going in a circle. Whoopee.

Next, we headed over to the carousel. The line encompassed the whole carousel, like a vortex of waiting people. We stood forever. I noticed there were more people in the park than when we started. A lot more. And it was getting hotter. By the time we got on the carousel, the surrounding area looked like a 1993 Pearl Jam mosh pit, if Pearl Jam played mostly to little kids and strollers.

Claire scrambled up on a black stallion while Kate needed a boost up on her white steed. The Better Half made all of us pose for pictures.

"You know our local zoo has this exact carousel. No line. Costs a dollar."

This comment elicited a glare of death that I did not find commensurate with pointing out a simple fact. I smiled and faced forward, knowing she would debate spending a dollar on that ride the next time we were at the zoo, even though we were spending the equivalent of one hundred dollars on this ride right now.

Right as we stepped off, a beautiful young girl dressed as Alice in Wonderland appeared. A giant white rabbit appeared next to her holding a pocket watch in one hand. My kids thought it was his giant cell phone. Handlers started pushing the crowd back. This was Pearl Jam.

We scurried into the quickly lengthening line for an autograph. The Better Half had bought "autograph books" at the local Dollar Store before we left, so we wouldn't have to buy the twenty-five-dollar official Disney ones in the gift shop. She had them sealed in the backpack in Ziploc bags with pens. And I fell in love all over again. This woman had just saved us forty-eight dollars.

When it was our turn, I just hoped Alice didn't try to have a moment with me, like Esmerelda did years ago. The white rabbit would have to step in, and it would all be very embarrassing. Alice looked at me and smiled with the same smile reserved for men who live to be one hundred years old in the nursing home. She quickly signed our autograph books, and a handler shoved us in front of the white rabbit. The rabbit fumbled with the autograph book and pen. That was easily forgiven because he had only three fingers on his costume, and it had to be one thousand degrees in that furry snowsuit. He got the autograph book set using his knees as support and signed "White Rabbit" in perfect calligraphy. Dang! That was some Disney magic.

We wandered back onto the midway. It was shoulder to shoulder and stroller to stroller. And steamy. We were headed for The Mad Hatter's Teacup Ride. There were so many people ... I couldn't even tell where the line began. As you entered the ride, strollers had to be given to one unlucky employee. He then ran them over to where you got off and kept them in the perfect order. We evolved over millennia from hunter-gatherers who walked over whole continents into fat slobs stuffed into Mickey T-shirts whose three-year-olds can no longer walk for themselves. And one unlucky Homo sapien spent his days sprinting with strollers. Wow.

We got to our teacup. The name held true. It was a ride in a teacup. The family slid into their seats, but I couldn't seem to get my left knee to join us. There were "you have to be this tall to ride" signs all over the park. Where was the "if you are taller than this, you will dislocate your knee on this ride" signs? I finally scooted my butt up the back of the bench seat and grimaced. The ride started, and every time someone turned the steering wheel in the middle, the whole teacup spun like a family-sized sit-and-spin. Kate turned it like a big rig trucker taking a corner. Laughing her head off. Everything was spinning, it was hot, and I felt like I was about to puke. But I knew I wouldn't. I'm too cheap. I paid fifty-eight dollars for breakfast.

I staggered off into a mosh pit of sweaty tourists. The Better Half was determined to take the kids on It's a Small World. She said she has fond memories of riding it as a little girl. I plead with her to let those memories suffice, to no avail.

We got close. I was going up to random people to learn where the line began.

"Are you in line?" I asked a fat lady in a pink Mickey shirt. She just scowled at me like I had tried to steal her last piece of bacon.

"Are you in line for Small World?" I asked an older gentleman.

"I thought we were going on some Peter Pan crap," he responded. "I don't know."

I found someone in line. He just pointed backwards. There were a lot of someones in line. The trout on my shirt started swimming upstream. I could barely see the entrance. Strollers swirled around me like sharks. We began the forever wait while The Better Half tried to beguile the girls with tales of how amazing this ride would be.

We finally got inside, and the feeling of shade on my body nearly sent me into shock. There were a thousand people in front of us in a switchback line. The toddler in front of me dropped his pacifier on the disgusting floor and started crying; the mom popped it right back in. The grandpa behind me looked old enough to have fought in World War II, and the look on his face said that the war was easier. We got to a sign that said it'd be thirty minutes more before we reached the start of the ride. I started to wonder how many people had died in this line. There had to be a few. We passed under a bridge that had a control tower on top. People wearing headsets were glaring out the windows with very serious looks like they were landing aircraft instead of watching boats on a conveyer belt.

We hopped on a boat. Either the boats were bigger, or I was smaller, a decade ago. I hoped I didn't make us capsize. We entered our first country with Styrofoam figures bouncing up and down to the music.

"Well, this is disappointing," said Kate.

"Boring," said Claire.

"Quiet, girls, we spent your college education money on this trip. Enjoy HVAC repair classes after high school," I whispered.

We popped back out on the crowded street. Shoving our way forward, the girls made it clear to the parental units that it was 12:02, and they were "starving." Up ahead, I saw some kind of Swiss village themed place with an archway you had to walk through. There was a courtyard and a line of food windows. On the left side of the archway were three stock Disney characters—a man dressed like a 17th century landowner and two girls wearing period dresses. The girls fawned over the guy, and all three broke into song. In a British accent. In Switzerland. The heavy set one sounded like Eliza Doolittle from *My Fair Lady*. No one was trying to get the autograph of these three, and from what I could tell, they were there just to distract us from the fact that this food court was a hot mess of sweaty tourists.

The courtyard had a few tables. There were people lined up awkwardly watching the people currently eating. Hovering over them, waiting to take their seat. Then there were people waiting on those people.

The Better Half and I glanced at each other and resigned ourselves to sitting on the curb under a construction sign. I hoped they were building more tables. I told her to try to secure us cement-curb seating while I got our food. I waded forward into the mob using a breaststroke action. I couldn't help but picture the Japanese commuter trains where police just shove more people on.

Again, I was forced to start the "Are you in line?" form of questioning. Angry looks helped me find my way. I am very tall, so I could look over the crowd and see there were ten food windows and about one hundred people in each line. So, there were one thousand people in these lines in the area the size of a school bus. Many of us were glaring at the jerks with strollers who took up three places in line. We were shoulder to shoulder, and it was not clear where the lines were and where to merge. I felt like I was in one of those prison shows and there was about to be violence in the yard. Someone was going to take one of these strollers, kid still in it, and go over some dad's head.

In the line to my right, two feet in front of me, was a pleasant couple and their son. The mother was in a wide-brimmed hat. The dad had a bad comb-over and was in khaki shorts and an ill-fitting polo. Standing between them was their gangly son who had dark hair and looked to be about fourteen. He stood awkwardly, not unlike a baby giraffe.

All of a sudden, baby giraffe crumpled to the ground. Passed out. His head couldn't hit the asphalt because of the crowd and came to rest on the shoes of the man behind him. Mom in the hat bent down and cradled his head. He was not responding to her voice. She started screaming for help, her husband's eyes darting from face to face.

No one moved. No one made eye contact. No one was giving up their place in line. Four hours of Disney brainwashing and a thousand people were ready to trade a boy's life for a place in line. Viktor Frankl didn't need to go to Auschwitz to learn about man's depravity; a couple of minutes in a food line at Disney would have done it.

I heard Eliza Doolittle's cockney accent behind me as the costumed woman came barreling through the lines. While singing. She stopped in front of the boy, hoisted her 17th century skirt in one hand while lifting her other hand to the heavens.

"What has happened here? What is going on here?" she sang. Yes, sang. In a British accent.

The mom was sobbing. She just looked up silently in a panic. Eliza shoved her way up to the ordering window. She slapped the metal counter to get the attention of a pimple-faced girl, who looked to be breaking child labor laws just by being there and had learned not to make eye contact with anyone.

"You need to call EMS. A boy has passed out and needs medical attention," she sang, using a higher octave for the word "attention." All in a British accent.

The cashier reached to her right and pulled a black corded telephone off the wall. I didn't even know corded phones still existed. The little boy to my right just stared at the phone, like he had seen an alien spaceship.

A minute later, a squad of four burly men in dark blue uniforms showed up. They had a stretcher with them. The lines didn't move to let them through. Every person just stared forward while outliers looked for a way to dart in.

Finally, the men started shoving their way through. They carefully placed the boy on the stretcher and started to carry him out, the sobbing mother right behind them. The father lingered. This nutjob didn't want to give up his spot in line. His wife grabbed his hand and pulled him away, the gap immediately closing.

I got to the window and ordered three mac and cheeses, four fries, four drinks, and a cheeseburger for me. The girl tapped at her register and never looked up.

"Sixty-eight."

I didn't even feign surprise. I was close to heat stroke and numb. I just handed over my credit card. A wave of her hand had me step to the right so she could take the next order. My arm touched the sweaty, hairy shoulder of some man in a tank top. With Mickey on it. I wanted to die.

I was never great at math. It's one of the reasons I majored in elementary education in college. That allowed me to take math-for-third-graders as my college math class. It was taught as though we were third graders. I didn't do all that well. But even I could look at these lines and realize this shack was making a million dollars at lunch. I decided I would buy Disney stock when we got home. Whatever the share price, it was undervalued.

Two overstuffed cup holders were shoved out the window. These weren't just my drinks; they were everything. Everything was served in a cup. Part genius. Part sixty-eight dollars insulting. My twelve-dollar cheeseburger was stuffed in a cup. I decided not to risk the condiment line and rejoined my family.

"What took so long? The girls are starving," stated The Better Half from her comfortable seat on the concrete curb.

I prepared to release a string of expletives that would make Donald Duck blush and explained in no uncertain terms that I watched someone almost die in line. Who needs ketchup when my hands are covered in blood? But I refrained and dug my cheeseburger out of a cup with my hands.

We finished eating in the blazing sun, sitting on a concrete curb, a construction privacy fence to our backs. I tried to peek through the cracks, expecting to see construction workers pushing wheelbarrows of cash from behind the food windows.

Our fearless leader, The Better Half, dragged us toward Adventureland. Personally, I had had enough adventure for the day. Kate fell to her knees and started to cry. Parents become very adept at identifying the different types of cries, much like a mechanic can diagnose an engine just by the whine or squeal it makes. And children become experts at choosing the correct volume and tone of a cry. In this art form, little Kate was Mozart.

Kate let out a long wail between breaths, letting me know this would not end quickly. I considered the threat of a spanking to shut the whole thing down. She was smart enough to call my bluff, knowing I would never make a memory of what would become known as: "That time you spanked me at Disney as I yelled for Mickey Mouse to save me."

The tone of the cry said she wanted something. We just had food and drinks. Her eyes darted to the street vendor in front of her. His cart was overflowing with sawdust-filled Disney characters and those personal fan/water bottles that I saw at the entrance and laughed at. I was not laughing now.

"If I could have one of those mister fans, it would be like having my own air conditioning," Kate said. "I could walk all day."

I could not believe I was considering spending thirty dollars on a bottle with a squirt gun and little fan attached ... with the obligatory Mickey sticker on the side. The spanking option started to seem more viable and cheaper. I looked to the penny-pinching Better Half for support, but she was too far gone.

"Just buy her the dang fan," she said.

I walked over to the cart and handed the teenage vendor my credit card. He smiled, because he saw kids checkmate their parents here all day long.

The little one misted her face, turned on the fan, and smiled a smug little smile. We stood in forever lines for two more rides and then decided to buy a Christmas ornament, I guess to commemorate the time Dad had spent thirty dollars on a stupid mister fan that was made in a foreign country for thirty cents. I repressed the next couple of hours because the next thing I remembered was that everyone in the park was now streaming back toward Main Street USA. It was dark and late.

The Better Half found another comfortable curb, and I was instructed to go get dinner. I crossed Main Street, which was now packed with people, and hit up Casey's Corner hot dog restaurant. The line started outside. I slowly made my way to the register. This place had drinks, hot dogs, and fries. The people around me fell into two distinct groups: those of us who had succumbed to this false economy where eighty dollars for hot dogs seemed like a reasonable deal, and the small remnant stuck in shock at the prices. The guy in front of me actually dropped the f-bomb in a distinct Brooklyn accent when the cashier mentioned his total. I really wanted to ask him where he had been all day. Is there a reasonably priced Disney I missed?

I ordered hot dogs, fries, and drinks. I handed over the credit card, numb to the fact that I would have to work weeks as a teacher and eat peanut butter sandwiches for lunch for a year to pay for this baseball stadium-themed meal. These folks had not figured out how to shove everything into a cup. I was forced to carry one bottle of water cinched in my teeth while my arms fumbled with the rest ... like I was trying to hold half a dozen puppies at once. Meanwhile, French fries flew from containers as other overburdened customers spun around from the counter, eager to get back to their tables ... or curbs. The workers behind the counter pretended not to see any of it.

I returned, and my family scarfed down the hot dogs and fries. A booming voice erupted from nowhere and told everyone to clear the road. We were forced to stand, and everyone was shoulder to shoulder. Disney employees roped off both sides of the main thoroughfare. No one was allowed to cross the street. Families were separated. I saw a dad on the other side, his arms full of hot dogs. His wife and kids were next to me. He yelled to them; the family had been split like refugees. He looked longingly at his kin, then he unwrapped one of the hot dogs and started eating.

The booming voice announced the Main Street Electrical Parade was about to begin. Float after float, decorated with coordinated flashing Christmas lights and accompanied by twirling dancers, went by as peppy music blared. I felt a tug on my shorts and looked down. The little one was standing with both arms outstretched.

"Pick me up so I can see better."

I fell for it and lift her up. She buried her head into my shoulder, facing away from the parade. Her fairy wings stuck in my face. I glanced down, and Claire was getting sleepy, each blink getting longer and longer. Kate started snoring into my shoulder.

"Everyone pay attention! This is the big finish! We paid a lot of money for you not to remember this!"

It was hopeless. Kate was asleep, and Claire was standing limp next to The Better Half like a zombie.

The parade ended, and fireworks lit up Cinderella's Castle. Big booms echoed off the buildings, and then it all ended with whoops and cheers from the crowd. I'll never forget Kate sleeping through it.

The river of people that carried us in now moved in the opposite direction. We flowed back out to the parking lot and its fifty busses, each purring in place. I was once again thankful for The Better Half as she remembers our bus number and stall. I would have gotten on the wrong bus and end up in Alabama.

The gentle hum of the bus engine and darkness had the packed bus silent. I had a sleeping Kate on my lap, and The Better Half was cradling Claire. We smiled at each other.

"Pretty magical," I whispered.

Without me doing anything, Kate's fairy wings sprung to life. The back of the bus was bathed in flashes of purple and green while a harmonious chime rung out. It was Disney magic.

Kate lifted her head at the sound.

"Why did you push the button?"

"I swear I didn't."

She sighed and buried her head into my shoulder and whispers, "This is the happiest place on Earth."

And at that moment, it was.

3
KATE (ALMOST) KILLS DAD

KATE BOOT CAMP

I'm going to be a father, again. Just as I would not show up at boot camp having never done a push-up, one should not bring another baby home without some drilling. Here are ten simple exercises I've developed to have a person mentally and physically prepared for child domination.

Take all of your kitchen utensils to your bed. Pull back your covers. Spread them out. Set your alarm clock for one minute in the future. Lie down and try to sleep. Do not shut off the alarm when it goes off. This will prepare you to have a child poking you and being loud in your bed. At some point, your spouse will bring in the baby, or it will crawl in on its own volition. Prepare now.

Take your alarm clock into the bathroom. Set the alarm for two minutes in the future. Sit on the toilet. Get comfortable, maybe read a magazine. When the alarm goes off, you're done. Definitely done.

Take all your belongings out of the house and put them in the driveway. Pack them all in your car. Won't fit? You will need more stuff than this for a weekend trip to Grandma's house. Quit lying to yourself and go buy a minivan.

Go to the mall and spend an hour picking out a gift for your sofa. But of course, your sofa wouldn't know what gift you got it, right? This is to prepare you for unsuccessful shopping trips and protracted conversations about what to buy a baby. You will also be shopping as if you're the baby buying presents for Mom. Never mind that a baby has no income and is ... a baby. Seriously.

Get a second job. Not just any second job, a second job that is harder than your current job and takes twice as long. Offer to do this job for free. Or better yet, offer to pay to do this second job. For the next eighteen years.

Buy a doll with scary eyes. The kind that never close or blink. Carry it everywhere you go. Make sure it is always looking at you. Even when you sleep, shower, and go to the bathroom.

Learn to survive on the following foods: macaroni and cheese, peanut butter and jelly, pizza, frozen waffles, and fruit snacks (these cannot contain actual fruit).

Learn to make deals like a car salesman at the end of the month. Practice constantly. Buying a new TV? See if you can get that sales guy to eat four bites of peas before you buy. Lady at work wants a donation to help cure cancer? See if you can get her to sit quietly in her chair for the next three minutes before considering a donation.

Draw a red line around the entire interior of your house. It should be 18 inches off the floor. Anything below the red line will be ruined. Move anything you value above the red line. The red line will move up 6 inches every year. For the next eighteen years.

Start practicing your countdown. Make threats and begin counting backwards from some random number. Eating dinner with the in-laws? Say something like, "If I don't have dessert on my plate by the time I get to one, somebody is going to time-out." Slow down the counting if you see your target responding. Speed it up if they do not.

KATE BORN ON THE BATHROOM FLOOR

Our first baby was a preemie. Born ten weeks early. The Better Half and I were supposed to watch a video detailing the steps of having a baby. We didn't get to that homework. We planned on birthing classes with our second, but I kept putting it off. Then, at thirty-eight weeks, our obstetrician scheduled an induction. Putting off the homework worked out, or so we thought.

The Better Half had heard some nasty rumors about being induced. There would be poles with fish hooks attached, a beach ball inflated somewhere, and the dreaded Pitocin. As she detailed her fears, I pretended none of this would happen and some bear-like creature would jump on her stomach one time like "Hop on Pop" and out would squirt a baby. Neither of us had any idea what a full-size baby coming out would be like.

Before her scheduled Monday induction, The Better Half went to her Friday morning ladies' Bible Study. She had asked the women to pray that she would not have to go through the medieval torture of being induced. That the baby would come on its own. I have since learned an important fact: When you ask the ladies of Bible Study to pray, you better be darn specific. Lest they unleash some super powerful prayers with unknown effects.

On Friday night, I am lying on the couch watching the Lakers game. The Better Half has checked all the boxes off her to-do list, despite the fact we are not going anywhere until Monday. Suitcases are packed and in the hallway. In-laws scheduled to arrive Sunday night. All ready to force this baby out on Monday morning.

The Better Half says her back hurts. I rub it while watching the game over her shoulder. She grabs a pen and paper and starts making a final list of baby names. My votes of Kobe and Shaq are shot down with an icy glare. We separately list our top three. One name overlaps. Kate it is.

The Better Half heads to bed. I decide to watch a little more of the game.

"My water just broke," she calls down to me with no sense of panic. Just prayers being answered. I consider finishing watching the game but decide to head upstairs to check on her. I've seen people have babies plenty on TV. We are going to drive to the hospital. Grueling hours of labor lie ahead. A skyscraper full of doctors and nurses will carefully monitor our progress, and in less than 24 hours, we'll have a new bouncing baby girl named Kate.

Good thing we never wasted our time learning about childbirth. We'd never need it. Once again, not doing homework works out in the end. I love you, procrastination.

I call my sister to come over to stay with two-year-old Claire and the dog. I help The Better Half strip the bed so we can wash the sheets. I run down to pull my SUV out of the garage and put the suitcases in the hatch. I'm just ambling through my checklist, happy my wife did not have to be induced, and humming to myself. I mosey back upstairs to our bedroom. The Better Half sticks her head out of our bathroom.

"Call 911!" she says, panicked.

"Are you sure? An ambulance ride is not going to be covered by insurance if it is not a true emergency. Remember, we've never had a full-size baby before. I'm sure you're fine."

"Does this look fine?"

The Better Half motions for my eyes to leave hers and glance down to where my brand-new baby daughter is attempting a perilous escape. I never did my "have-a-baby" homework, but I know a giant head coming out when I see it.

I fumble with the phone while pressing 911. I am certain the look on my face is similar to when you mean to pass gas and accidently poop yourself instead. The Better Half mirrors the look, but she is about to squirt out a baby accidently. Pooping herself is also a real possibility. (I'd have known that if I had learned about childbirth.) I say "squirt" because I have absolutely no idea how this is supposed to happen.

"My wife is in labor. We need an ambulance," I say calmly to the 911 operator. But in my mind, I am freaking out. The dispatcher matches my calmness and assures me paramedics are on their way. My house is very close to the fire station. I could jog there. A few minutes creep by, and The Better Half lays down on the bathroom floor. I hear silence on the phone. I start to lose it.

"I'm not hearing any sirens!" I say louder than before.

"They are on their way," the dispatcher calmly assures me.

"If they were 'on their way,' they'd be here!"

"They are on their way," she answers calmly as trained, I'm sure. Another minute creeps by; The Better Half moans.

"LISTEN LADY, THERE IS GOING TO BE A BABY WIGGLING ON THIS BATHROOM FLOOR REALLY SOON!" I scream into the phone.

"Hello?" I hear from downstairs. Feet slowly pound up the stairs, and I hear a chuckle. What could be funny? They just don't know the situation. Once they see, they will spring into action. The cavalry is here. Medical professionals. I hear them discussing how to get the gurney up the stairs. No panic or concern in their voices.

A young girl who looks like a college student—probably one who has two first names like Ashley Kate—sticks her head in the bathroom. She is followed by two middle-aged men who look like your prototypical firefighters named Chuck and Buck or something, guys who come from generations of firefighters. Last, there is the old man who drove the ambulance.

They looked at me, looked at The Better Half splayed out on the floor with a baby crowning, and all got the same look on their faces. It was like four people meant to pass gas and all crapped themselves. We had a real crapstorm blowing up that bathroom. Without one person speaking, everyone was aware that not one of us knew anything about having a baby. This was going to be problematic. Especially for the lady groaning on the floor.

Having a heart attack? Suburban EMTs are your saviors. Cut your toes off in the lawnmower? Suburban EMTs will get those little piggies on ice and get you to the hospital. Car wreck? EMTs are getting out the Jaws of Life and prying you out. Accidentally having a baby on the bathroom floor? You're screwed. Turns out they make runs like this all the time. People think they are having a baby, and they are not. They put the mom-to-be on a gurney, take her to the hospital, and hours later, a baby is born. So is a fight with the insurance company about an unneeded ambulance ride. No one actually, accidentally, has a baby on the bathroom floor. But we are.

"Maybe you better go get the 'Have a Baby Kit' out of the truck," says Chuck to Buck.

WHAT? I scream in my mind. There's a kit for this? Is it next to the Accidentally Cut Off Toe in Lawnmower Kit? Or next to the

Heimlich Maneuver Kit? Which contains nothing. A kit? Does it have a bullet and a little vial of whiskey?

And did he just say "truck?" I did not know they called the ambulance a truck. I pictured a 1986 Silverado in my driveway. Right now, that would not surprise me.

It quickly became obvious that no one present wanted anything to do with the situation happening on the floor. We all just looked at each other for a second like poker players with a pair of deuces. Ashley Kate flinched first, inching her way back out of the doorway and bumping into Buck, coming back with the "Have a Baby Kit." It contained a plastic sheet, bulb syringe, and small scalpel. Was the scalpel for one of these amateurs to do an emergency C-section? No help at all.

Chuck and Buck kneel down on the floor in front of The Better Half and feign knowledge of what to do. One grabs the "Have a Baby Kit" and pulls out the bulb syringe, like that is something important right now.

"Don't forget your breathing," Ashley Kate calls out from the other room. The Better Half politely screams at her with the voice of a demon that we never did our homework or studied breathing techniques.

In my mind, I just start thinking of escape plans. My SUV is still in the driveway with the hatch open. I could grab The Better Half and throw her in the back. They just opened a new hospital two miles from our house. They might know how to have a baby there. I could Google this situation. Surely someone has been through this and made a how-to video. No, I'll probably get a bunch of memes showing a nerdy guy's face that says: "Wife having baby on floor. Never did his homework on childbirth." Focus. Think of every TV show where they had a baby. What did they do? Lay them down and encourage pushing. That's all I got. And that's what the EMTs were already doing.

The Better Half let out a scream and started panting. This is happening. For a split second, there is silence. Chuck kneels on the floor, hands at the ready like a catcher covering home plate. The rest of the baby's head pops out. Buck, with his bulb syringe, stabs at a nostril. Chuck grabs his arm. "I don't think we do that yet," he whispers.

I am silently praying for a sign of life. Anything. This baby is never going to meet her dad because he is going to die of a heart attack hoping she breathes. The room goes still.

All of a sudden, my daughter takes a big breath. So does the rest of the room. We all start cheering on The Better Half. All she needs is one more big push and it's all over. I kneel down next to her ear. "You got this!"

There is something none of us know in our encyclopedic knowledge of having babies. Someone is supposed to reach inside there and turn the shoulders of this baby. She's ready to hit that opening like a Mack truck ramming a mouse hole.

We all cheer on The Better Half. She strains and screams. We cheer, not knowing she is getting ripped in half. After all, the people on TV shows scream. This is how it's supposed to go, right?

Then a baby actually does squirt out. Who knew? We all congratulate each other for a few minutes. Ashley Kate, standing in the back, scoops up the baby, and Buck finally gets to use his bulb syringe. We figure out the intended purpose of the scalpel, and I cut the cord. It's surprisingly rubbery, almost like a garden hose. It takes me two tries.

"Do you have a bath towel to wrap the baby in?" asks Ashley Kate.

"Yeah, check the cabinet right behind you. Should be a clean one on the bottom," answers the postpartum lady lying on the floor, concerned about the cleanliness and organization of her bathroom. Ever the hostess.

"What time was she born?" asks Ashley Kate.

Silence.

Ashley Kate makes up a time, and we all nod in agreement. They roll The Better Half down the stairs, Ashley Kate trailing with my newborn swaddled in a dark blue bath towel.

We all get to the hospital. It is two minutes from the house, and it just opened. It has a new-car smell. They roll The Better Half into a delivery room and carefully transition her onto a birthing table. I wonder what these idiots are doing. Are the nurses as new as the hospital? All of a sudden, one of the nurses pauses.

"I don't think we need to be in this room," she states.

Duh! What gave it away, the fact that Ashley Kate is standing next to you with my newborn daughter in a blue bath towel? They transition The Better Half back onto the gurney and send us to a recovery room. New baby goes under a heat lamp and gets a stocking cap. I've never seen a new baby not in an aquarium. She looks huge. How did that come out of my wife?

A nurse practitioner comes in to stitch up The Better Half. She explains the turning of the shoulders idea to me, just in case we ever accidently give birth on the bathroom floor again. While interjecting a, "Wow, she really ripped you a new one," every once in a while.

We wait in the recovery room for them to admit us. And wait. And wait. After about an hour, a nerd comes into the room and calls me out into the hallway. He is actually wearing a pocket protector and glasses with a piece of tape on them. He calmly explains that they are a paperless hospital, and everything is run on computer. They need the computer to print a special bracelet to be attached to my daughter's leg to admit her. The computer will not accept a time of birth before a hospital admittance time. It just spits out error codes. They have an emergency call in to a programmer in Cincinnati. I picture his twin getting the call and getting out of bed, already dressed exactly as he is now.

"Just put in a time of birth after the time of admittance. We just made up the time of birth anyway," I answer.

Nerd's head explodes. He says that would be wrong. And the hospital would charge us for a birth. And the time on our birth certificate would be wrong.

"Fine. Just admit us without the bracelet."

Nerd huffs and puffs. That violates hospital protocol. They had spent thousands on special sensors that would sound alarms if anyone tried to leave with that bracelet. Like my baby was a pair of expensive jeans at Target.

"There's no one else in your nursery. And my baby is the one in the blue bath towel. I'm feeling pretty safe," I respond, to his chagrin.

An hour later, he lies about the time of birth and gets us our bracelet. Nothing like frustration at two in the morning to make you cave on your morals. Technology: making people worse by the day.

We settle into our room. Baby is safe and secure in the nursery, alone. This new hospital has a pull-down TV with a touchscreen menu and a wonderful pull-out bed for me. As I drift off to sleep, I smile. I never learned anything about having a baby. Never did my homework. Everything ended up fine. Procrastination wins again.

And the hospital charged us for a delivery.

We have been teaching Kate simple sign language so she can better communicate since she only says one word: dog. An example from tonight's dinner:

Me (making the sign for more): Kate, make the sign for more if you want more.

Kate: Dog.

Me (making the sign for all done): You done? Make the sign.

Kate (pointing at the dog): Dog.

Me: We are not getting another dog.

Kate screams and throws her food on the floor.

I was sitting on my bed after school, and two-year-old Kate walks in naked.

Me: Where are your clothes?

Kate: I dunno. Potty.

Me: You want to sit on the potty like a big girl? Great!

Kate (on the potty and contorting her head downward): PEE PEE, WAKE UP!

Me: I don't think this is how potty training works. I used candy with your sister.

Kate: PEE PEE, WAKE UP!

Me: Or we can stick with this. Wake up, pee pee.

Kate: Can I have a banamo?

Me: Not until you learn to say banana. Repeat after me.

Kate: Okay.

Me: BA

Kate: BA

Me: NAN

Kate: NAN

Me: NA

Kate: MO. Got it!

Me: Here's your banamo. Enjoy.

Kate: I have to poop.

Me: Like right now?

Kate: It's kinda peeking out.

Me: That counts as right now.

Dear Essential Oils,

    Why don't you develop an oil I can rub on my daughter's feet that will stop her from spilling glitter all over my house. That I would buy.

                              Dad

―――――――

Me: Kate, you stay in bed tonight. I would hate for you to have to get a spanking tonight for getting out of bed.

Kate: Who is doing the spanking? You or Mommy?

Me: Why?

Kate: If it's Mommy, I'm getting out of bed.

Me: It's me.

Kate: Hmmmm ... Well, good night. See you in the morning.

―――――――

Toilet-side Conversation:

Kate: Do you know why I wuv you, Daddy?

Me: Why is that?

Kate: 'Cause you always sit and talk to me when I go poop.

Me: Maybe I just like sitting here on the edge of the bathtub. Ever think of that?

Kate: No, you wuv me. Here comes a big one.

―――――――

Tonight is bittersweet. Tomorrow is Kate's birthday. She will be three. I just rocked my two-year-old to sleep for the last time. A treasured moment. I often wonder what thoughts will cloud my mind as I take my last breath here on Earth. Rocking Kate might be what I remember. I want to do this forever.

———

Me: If I buy you these ruby red high heels, you're going to want to wear them everywhere with every outfit. Your mom will be so mad at me.

Kate: So, can I get them?

Me: I don't see why not.

Dear Kate,

They are candy canes, not "hookers." They do have a hook shape, so I see how you could get confused. When you said, "I'm going to get daddy a hooker for Christmas," I knew what you meant. I'm afraid some innocent bystander may get the wrong idea about our family values.

                                      Thanks,

                                      Management

Kate: It's snowing out. Guess who is coming back?
Me: It's February. Not Santa.
Kate: SANTA!

Playing hair stylist is one of many games such as doctor and the deathly ill, or dead body and the detective, that involve me collapsed on the couch. Kate is perched on the arm of the couch, brush in hand.
Kate: Some of your hair on top has decided to ummmm ... retire.

Kate: Let's talk about who has pecs and who has boobies.
Me: What?

Kate: You have pecs; Mommy has boobies. I have boobies, and my friend Aaron has pecs. Bob has pecs, and Lisa has boobies. Do you see how it works?

Me: I've gotten pretty out of shape. I might be in the booby category now.

———————

Kate: I think you should never spank me again. My bottom might break.

Me: It already has a crack. Ha!

Kate: I don't get it.

Me: That's okay. I've only been waiting my whole life to use that line on one of my kids, and it flops. I literally had kids so I could tell that joke.

———————

Swimming instructor: That Kate is very strong-willed.

Me: That is a kind way to put it. We call her "the reason we're not having more kids."

———————

Kate: When you talk to me, you say, "My Damn."

Me: Young lady, I don't know where you have heard this kind of language but …

Kate: I'm a princess and must be called "My Damn."

Me: Oh! You mean madam. Yes, of course, madam.

Kate: What did you think I said?

Me: Nothing. Madam.

Me: Kate, how did you get this red mark on your neck?

Kate: I got stung by a bee.

Me: Seriously?

Kate: Just kidding. Actually, I was choked by an owl.

Me: Today is a snow day. It is very cold. Choose an outfit that will keep you nice and warm.

Kate: Princess dress!

Me: That is not going to keep you warm enough. Bare arms and legs. Brrrrrr.

Kate: I'll add a cape.

Car Seat Conversation

Kate: Dad! Stop the car! One of my car seat buckles is not clicked in!

Me: Relax. I'll reach back and click it at the next stoplight.

Kate: Okay. I'll keep an eye out for the cops. If they see us breaking the law, you will be in super big trouble.

Me: I'll fix it in one minute.

Kate: I will visit you in prison, Dad. I'll miss you. I'll still love you.

———

Kate: Today, I am a snake. I might bite you. Sssssssss.

Me: Ummmm, snakes don't talk.

Kate: Ummmm, ever read the Bible?

Me: Well played, little girl. Well played.

———

Kate: What do I need to do to get a special treat after dinner?

Me: Eat those last three bites.

Kate: Okay. I'm going to unbutton the top button on my pants and then lie on the couch, and you rub my back.

Me: That seems like a lot for three small bites.

Kate: I'll be on the couch.

———

Kate: Dad, you ever think about if someone made you small, and mashed you up, and put you in batter, and made pancakes out of you, and ate you with butter and syrup?

Me: I never once thought of that.

Kate: I think you would be delicious. 'Cause you're my sweet daddy.

We were with extended family trying to figure out where Kate got her dark brown eyes. No one in our families have eyes that dark.

Me: Where did you get those beautiful dark brown eyes?

Kate: Jesus.

THE KATE WORKOUT

The newest craze sweeping the nation is finally at your doorstep. Special delivery. How would you like a workout that is especially designed to exhaust and, maybe, kill you? A product that will not quit? Let me introduce you to a special weight training system. This is not available in stores, at least not in this country. But you can make one with items readily available in your bedroom. People even acquire them by accident. It's the product your mother-in-law has pestered you about. Introducing: The Kate.

Quads: Squat down and pick up all twenty-four pounds of The Kate. Get full extension. Feel the burn. If you accidently drop The Kate, an alarm will sound for the next thirty minutes. All while The Spouse belittles you. After about twenty seconds of holding The Kate, she will start to wiggle and demand to be put down. Squat back down and carefully set the weight on the floor. Relax. The Kate will immediately want to be picked up again. Repeat one thousand times a day.

Abs: The Kate has the ability to come crashing down on your stomach at any time. Often, this will include jumping off things and onto your belly like a wrestler coming off the top buckle. Fall asleep on the couch watching football? Here comes the ab crusher. Attempting to deflect The Kate by putting up the knees can result in a hit to the groin. Just grin and take it. A reprimand will have no effect.

Grandma and Grandpa will think it's cute. Tickling may remove the threat, but only temporarily.

Biceps and Lats: Squat down like you are going to the bathroom, because you are. Now reach out with your right arm and hold the bathroom door shut while all the weight of The Kate is pulling in the opposite direction. That is not just you grunting and groaning. The Kate is designed to be with you always. Always. Hold a magazine in your opposite hand and try to detach yourself from the situation.

Shoulders and Back: In this exercise, The Kate demands to see the world, and you are obliged to make that happen. You lift her up onto your shoulders. Grab the two dangling appendages with your hands and hang on. The two upper appendages will automatically adhere to your hair. The Kate will demand you walk and then run. The Kate will control you by pulling your hair and kicking you like a jockey on the home stretch. Soon your clavicle and upper back will burn. The Kate will demand to be put down. And then put back up. Warning: Don't get The Kate laughing or crying. If The Kate gets too excited, it will release liquid down the back of your neck.

Full Body: Without warning, The Kate will start hurtling toward something harmful: an open flame, traffic, or a grandparent with candy. With no warm-up, you must sprint and win this race to danger. The race can begin in the backyard, at the mall, or even in the middle of the night. Once winning the race, grab The Kate and do a full squat. Reprimand The Kate. This will have no effect whatsoever and may trigger another race.

Attachments: A purchase of The Kate Training System will require buying several corresponding items. The Pack 'n Play attachment requires lifting a fifteen-pound oblong object and carrying it whenever you go somewhere for more than an hour. Setting it up includes a puzzle feature. An eight-pound Shoulder Bag must be carried at all times when you leave the house. It contains everything you will need, but you will be unable to locate the items without shoving your hand to the bottom like it is a bucket of rice. Last, there is the High Chair. This attachment must be pulled and pushed all over the kitchen and even carried down into the basement. Note: If these attachments are ever sold and another The Kate is ordered, they must all be repurchased. Keep the attachments in the basement forever and tell yourself that you are saving them for grandkids.

Diet: The Kate will eat at least half of any dessert you purchase. She will lick ice cream right off the cone and send it to the ground. Ants will get more dessert than you will. The Kate will slap healthy food right out of your hand and sound an immediate alarm. The Kate may even offer you a "bite" of its dessert, only to pull it back at the last second and consume it alone. Laughing. Remember, this training works. The Mom was able to drop over seven pounds, all in one big push, thanks to The Kate. And we can all agree that she had really ballooned in the nine months prior.

Separate Purchase: We now offer The Pup for the pugilist who wants a real workout. This fur-covered ball of fun is guaranteed to add a whole other level to your daily workouts. The Pup grows much faster than The Kate, and diapers are not an option.

Me: The temperature outside is below zero. Why did you put a bathing suit under your clothes?
Kate: Because it is DELICIOUS!
Me: I don't think that means what you think it means.

Me: This is from a lady at my work. She sent you a Christmas cookie.
Kate: What does a pink Darth Vader head have to do with Christmas?

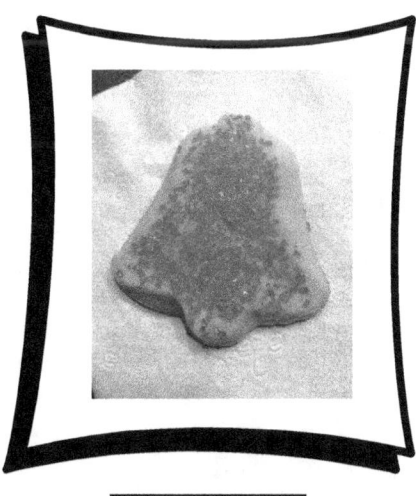

Kate: Dad, you still have big muscles in your arms. Your body is still young.

Me: Thank you, sweetie.

Kate: Except for your face. That is looking really old.

———

Kate: I know how to make our house safe from bad guys.

Me: How?

Kate: Just make it out of flowers. Boys hate flowers and girly stuff. They just like ninjas and fighting stuff. Bad guys wouldn't even go near a house made of flowers.

———

Kate: You ever ride a Miracle Around when you were a kid?

Me: It's called a Merry-Go-Round.

Kate: America Round. Got it.

———

Me: I thought I told you to eat your whole cupcake and not just lick all the frosting off the top.

Kate: A big fly landed on it. He licked off all the frosting and flew away. I think I heard him laughing.

Me: Did he happen to kiss you before he left?

Kate: Maybe. Why?

Me: You have frosting all over your lips.

Me: This is so fun! I have been dreaming of taking you sledding! I am so glad we have a snow day.

Kate: I'm cold. I want to go home. I got snow in my gloves.

Me: Awwwww … c'mon. This is so fun! We need to go at least ten more times.

Kate: I can't feel my lips. Can I just wait in the car?

This conversation happened. Except, to be honest, I spoke the words of Kate. And she the words of me.

Kate: I am completely full. Can't eat another bite.

Me: Then no room for dessert?

Kate: Let me explain how my body is different. I have five stomachs. One breakfast. One lunch. One snack. One dinner. One dessert.

Me: Are you a cow?

Kate: A cow ready for ice cream.

Kate: I have been thinking about who I am going to marry. I am going to marry you, Dad.

Me: I am already married to your mom.

Kate: I thought about that. And well, she's not going to live forever.

Me: Please don't kill your mom.

I told Kate she was going with me to a baby shower for a person I work with that she knows. Her name is Brianna. Leading to this conversation:

Kate: Mom, I am going to a birthday party for Brianna!

Me: It's not a birthday party. It is a baby shower. And it's a surprise. So, quit telling everyone. Brianna doesn't even know.

Kate: She doesn't know she's having a baby? This WILL be a surprise party!

Kate: I looked out in our yard, and I saw someone has glittered.

Me: Runaway fairies? Rainbow Bright?

Kate: No. Someone put trash in our yard. They glittered.

Me: It's called littered. Or Tinkerbell is a Stinkerbell.

Watching the news with Kate.

Kate: Why are those people shooting guns?

Me: They are involved in a war.

Kate: Oh, I could end that real fast.

Me: You could end conflict in the Middle East? Just how would you do that?

Kate: Lightsabers.

———

Kate: Dad, I think I'm ready to get baptized.

Me: I don't think you are ready. You're only five.

Kate: I'm not going to wear one of those white robes. I'm wearing my swimsuit. And when the preacher is done, I'm going to swim around a bit.

Me: As I was saying …

———

Kate was having a hard time in Sunday School, so she sat with me in church while her mom worked in the nursery. Leading to this Car Seat Conversation:

The Better Half: How was big church today?

Kate: It was fine. We stood up. Sat down. Sang songs. Oh, and Dad ate Jesus's body.

———

Me: I know you love to wear that ballerina dress, but at four I think it is time to retire it. You are getting a bit big to wear it.

Kate: Yeah. I was eating lunch with the babysitter, and my boob popped out.

Me: Were you in public?

Kate: No. I was in Wendy's.

———————

Kate: Let me get this straight. If I have a kid, you would be their grandpa?

Me: Correct.

Kate: Well, you better work on being more fun. Grandpas are fun. You'd be one boring grandpa.

Me: Thanks.

———————

Me: Kate, why are you staring at me making your sister's lunch? What's so thrilling about peanut butter and jelly?

Kate: When you put the two pieces together, it is so exciting! They kiss, and then they are married!

Me: I'm going to throw some animal crackers in her lunch box next.

Kate: Those can be their kids. Yes!

———————

In the grocery store, Kate is trying to shove a giant package of Charmin toilet paper into my cart.

Me: What are you doing?

Kate: Buy this one. A commercial on TV said it wipes so well that you can wear your same underwear for two days. Seriously.

Me: Enough said. We're buying it.

The 5-year-old is obsessed with Darth Vader. She loves him. So, I'm letting her watch *Star Wars*. In the beginning, Vader is interrogating Princess Leia. I hear her whisper, "Just kill her."

We went to Disney World. While there, Kate achieved her lifelong dream of meeting the real Darth Vader.

Disney Handler: No hugging Vader. Don't worry. No one tries to hug him. He's a bad guy.

Me: You never met my daughter. The Force is strong in her. The Dark Force, that is.

Then she hugged Darth Vader.

KATE KILLS SLEEP

I stumble out of my house toward my driveway on shaky legs. The sun won't be up for an hour, and the crisp air bites at my ears. My trembling hand can barely get the key in the ignition. I drag my sleeve across my snotty nose and try to focus. My head is throbbing. If I can just get the car on the road, it will drive itself. I need one more hit. To function. Just for today.

"Tomorrow I am stopping this," I whisper to myself, lying.

I can barely keep the car in my lane. A wave of depression crashes over me. I should be sitting down to a bowl of cereal. Not out at this ungodly hour. I have no appetite. It's not food my body craves.

As I turn into my dealer's drive, I wonder how I got here. A dad in his late thirties, leaving the house in darkness for a date with the devil. I pull up, and my dealer is waiting for me as always.

"Welcome to Starbucks. What can I get started for you?"

"Venti mocha double shot with whip," I say while pondering how I got to the point of paying five dollars for a hot milkshake with a hint of coffee. Then I remember how.

Three fateful nights.

I used to sleep like a champ. Like a hibernating grizzly bear. I would go to bed at midnight and barely wake up for lunch the next day. I remember, with fondness, rushing home from work to get in an afternoon nap before dinner. I should have kept sleep pants next to where I hung up my coat.

Coffee? I had no taste for the bitter bean. And I mocked those who did. Until those three fateful nights.

The first night came several years after their arrival. The kids, that is. As had become my usual parenting bedtime routine, I put them to bed, then I stumbled into my room, threw my clothes on the floor, and collapsed into a coma.

After what seemed like minutes of sleep, I felt sweat in my hair, and the whole left side of my face was wet despite it being the dead of winter. I wiped my brow, and for some unknown reason, I smelled my hand. It stunk of urine. Straight pee.

Still groggy, I immediately wondered how I had peed on my own face?

I looked to my left and realized two-year-old Kate had decided to join us in bed, just as her mother had trained her to do from birth. Somehow, The Better Half, a contract lawyer, got "Co-sleep with your baby" from the hospital handout that clearly stated, "Don't co-sleep with your baby." You get married and invite a woman into your bed. You do not realize you also get kids, dogs, and anything else that wanders in.

I quickly pieced it together. Kate had rolled between us and turned sideways, face near her mom's, probably had mom in a headlock. I was on my usual sliver of mattress, clueless. She sprawled across all the pillows—regular and decorative—and from that throne, peed. Right on my pillow. Only mine. Then she rotated back toward her mom. I rolled left—game over.

"Ahhhhhh, this is disgusting!" I screamed as I jumped up. "Who does this? Who pees on their parent's head?"

The Better Half slowly rose from her slumber, unconcerned, as her husband drowned in urine. In complete darkness, she deftly stripped the two-year-old and the bed. I do not believe she opened her eyes. The Better Half has horrible eyesight, and I had long suspected some kind of echolocation ability as an adaptation.

I headed for the shower while the two-year-old strolled, nude, back to her own room to get new pajamas and crawl back into her own, unsoiled, bed.

I returned from my shower, threw sweatpants on, and stood at the foot of my still stripped bed. The Better Half had taken the remaining unsoiled comforter and pillows and cocooned herself in them. Snoring. I went over to my barren sliver of mattress, laid down, and stared at the ceiling. Shivering. The clock said 3:50.

"How have I angered you, Oh Lord, that this is my fate?" I whispered into the darkness.

Silence.

So, I began my day. I walked downstairs and started making some breakfast, resigned to the fact that I would just have to survive down a night's sleep. I poured a bowl of cereal and considered giving in to the bitter bean. We had a coffee maker, purchased for when the in-laws visited. They downed the stuff by the pot. I was unsure how the contraption worked. Instead, I had Lucky Charms in a mixing bowl. Massive amounts of sugar would substitute for caffeine.

Imagine watching a zombie movie, and one of the zombies decides eating people is not for him, so he gets into a car and drives to work as a junior high teacher. That was me. I recall driving on a country road when what seemed like a reasonable thought went through my head: This road is pretty straight. I'll just close my eyes for a minute or two. A little nap.

A nap. While driving.

I snapped out of it and shook my head. I rolled down the window and blasted the radio. I usually listened to NPR in the morning, but that would just hasten thoughts of sleep. Eighties rap it was. Snap. I got the power. I considered getting a coffee from the McDonald's drive-through. But I resisted. I pulled into my parking place at work and just sat there, gripping the steering wheel.

The second night that led to my addiction was the very next night. I went to bed early, smiling, as I had not needed the bean to survive. I had made it. I fell into a deep slumber.

I awoke, no alarm needed. Because Kate was kicking me in the back. Squinted at the clock. Six thirty. I used the restroom, shaved, and brushed my teeth. I got dressed, thankful Kate had not peed on my head during the night. I was adjusting my sweater vest when The Better Half rolled over to face me.

"What are you doing?"

"Getting ready for work. What's it look like I'm doing?" I answered in the snarky tone reserved for a spouse.

The Better Half grabbed her clock and held it one inch from her face, mouth open. She was probably reading the numbers using her sonar.

"It's not six thirty in the morning. It's three thirty," she said while flopping over and returning to slumber.

I was shocked. How could one be so tired as to lose three hours of sleep and not even notice? I was already up and my anxious mind would not allow me to fall back to sleep. I slumped toward the kitchen, resigned to another day as a zombie. I poured a bowl of sugar cereal and got out the coffee maker. I retrieved coffee grounds and inspected the machine. Where would coffee go? Where does the water go? With a 50/50 chance of getting it wrong, I gave up and went to work.

I distinctly remember a student standing at my desk. How I got to that desk is still a mystery.

"What do you want?" I asked in an annoyed tone.

"May I use the bathroom?"

"Yes. Why didn't you just ask that, instead of standing there?"

"I did ask. Three times."

The third night that led to my addiction, I got home and somehow fixed something resembling dinner. I was down two nights of sleep. I collapsed into bed and into a deep slumber. Again, I awoke without my alarm. I rolled over and Kate was staring right into my face like some kind of zombie. I shuddered, and still half asleep, prepared for death. I had a good run.

I snapped out of it and looked at the clock. I pulled it next to my face. I looked again. I traced each number with my finger. Then I got ready for work.

I was adjusting my belt when The Better Half rolled over.

"What are you doing?"

"What's it look like I'm doing? It is six thirty. I triple checked," I said in a smart aleck tone reserved for a spouse when one is correct and sure of it.

I pointed at her clock and smiled.

"It's Saturday," she answered with the tone of resignation reserved for a spouse who had long realized she'd made a poor choice of a marriage partner.

"Would you like me to make you a coffee?" I asked, "'cause I'm DEFINITELY having one."

And that is how I became addicted to coffee.

Me: We need to work on your pronunciation. Say spaghetti.

Kate: Spell pasghetti.

Me: Looks like we both have some work to do. Postponed.

Me: What is your favorite color?

Kate: Rainbow.

Me: How was your first day of kindergarten?

Kate: We already have people not following the rules.

Me: Who?

Kate: Boys.

Me: Kate, you are doing so well in kindergarten. I bet you are reading by Christmas!

Kate: Reading minds? Because that is my real goal.

Kate: I think I'm ready to be baptized at church.

Me: I don't think so. You still think Rudolph might have been at Jesus's birth?

Kate: I'm just saying there were a lot of animals there, and Rudolph could be sneaky.

Kate: Dad, in school, I am coloring in the lines, and these kids at my table are just scribbling. Like animals!

Me: Just do your best. And encourage them to do better.

Kate: They are hopeless.

Me: Why do you say that?

Kate: They're boys.

Kate (as we walk into a donut shop): I might apply for a job while we are in here. Pretend you don't know that all I would do is eat donuts until I puke.

Me: Your secret is safe with me.

Kate: At recess, I got married to this boy named Brady.

Me: What's his last name?

Kate: I don't know. Do you have to know that?

Me: Yep.

Kate: Man, being married is hard.

Kate: Look what I found drawn in this book. A cartoon naked butt! Ha! Ha!

Me: I would like you to read books at your level.

Kate: Naked butts are my level.

_____

Kate: Today, in school, we had to guess how many seeds are in a pumpkin. I said fifty. One person said two and one person said infinity. Guess who made those other guesses.

Me: Boys?

Kate: Dumb. Dumb. Boys.

_____

Kate: I know what I will be when I grow up. A queen. A drama queen.

Me: Oh boy.

Kate: I'm going to be the type of lady that wears high heels, even in the snow.

_____

Car Seat Conversation

Kate: When cops pull people over to check for drinking, how do they check?

Me: They make them walk a line without falling over, close their eyes and touch their nose, count backwards.

Kate: Well, I would be going to jail.

———————

Kate: We can never go see our cousins that live with the vampires.

Me: They live in Pennsylvania. Not Transylvania.

Kate: Better not risk it.

SEVEN REASONS WHY WE CAN'T HAVE ANOTHER KATE

The Better Half has decided that maybe we should have another child. I have developed some arguments against this.

When I was a kid, I often watched professional wrestling. My friends and I would argue as to its authenticity. There was a legitimate move where one wrestler could lean out of the ring and "tag" another wrestler to jump in, and together, they would devise some torturous move to decimate the guy in the middle. Between my two girls, I am the guy in the middle getting his butt kicked. I bet the poor soul being tortured in a double suplex never thought, "I wish there was another person in here." Yeah. I don't think that either.

In my head, there is a countdown clock. It is currently at 3 years, 7 days, 5 hours, and 43 seconds. This is when I can finally go to the bathroom alone. No one yelling through the door, jiggling the handle, reaching tiny fingers under the door, or asking, "What are you doing in there?" like it is some kind of Nancy Drew mystery. Starting the clock over would kill me.

They recalled our crib. I'm not buying another. According to the manufacturer, our car seats have all expired. How does plastic expire? With my luck, a new baby would be a boy. All our baby clothes are for girls. I'm not buying more. That means our boy would have to be dressed like a girl, sleep in a dresser drawer, and ride in an expired car seat.

I never really learned what a "mucus plug" is. I never will.

If things continue at the current pace, college will cost $164,192 per child. Oddly, this is the exact price of a kidney on the black market. So, The Better Half could give one. I could give one. But we wouldn't have any other spare organs between us to send a third child to college.

One day, I would like to buy a new car. There are currently two hundred and eleven different models for sale. If we have a third child, three car seats would not line up across the back of most of those cars. That would leave an SUV as a choice. But those are expensive and get poor gas mileage. That would mean buying a minivan. There are eight to choose from, and only two are any good. I go from more than two hundred car choices to just two.

We could have twins.

Kate: Dad, you're really the only boy I can see myself marrying. And I have really thought about this.

Me: Why?

Kate: Boys are disgusting. They pee all over the bathroom. Have bad breath. Stinky armpits. Wear dirty clothes. Never shower. Take giant poops. And you're the only nice one I have ever met.

Me: I am strangely flattered. Love you.

Kate begged me to take her to the local park so she could show me what she learned at basketball camp. Faking an injury to steal the ball. That is what she learned.

Took the girls to the mall. Is it just me, or is Claire's a Spencer Gifts for ten-year-olds? We went to a store called Justice. Kate picked out a black leather jacket, leading to this conversation.

Kate: Give me one reason you won't buy me this.

Me: How about two. It is 95 degrees outside. And you are not in a first-grade off-Broadway revival of *Grease*.

Me: That is a cute little jumper you picked out to wear today.

Kate: To go to the bathroom, I have to take off all my clothes.

Me: Well, that seems like a design flaw.

———————

Kate: I'm the smart daughter.

Me: You are both equally silly.

Kate: The other one just packed sunscreen. For an indoor pool.

Me: You can be the smart one. Today.

———————

I was helping Kate hang up her clothes in her closet.

Me: What the heck kind of shirt is this?

Kate: It has a sports bra built in.

Me: What? You're seven. What would you need that for?

Kate: Right now, it's a sweat collector. But someday …

Me: Stop. I've heard enough.

———————

Kate: Do not steal my Halloween candy tonight. I worked hard collecting it.

Me: You're confused. You live here the other three hundred sixty-four days, so I can steal your candy. That's why I created you.

Kate: You love me. Not candy.

Me: I love Reese's Peanut Butter Cups.

Kate: I bet Rapunzel had a serious problem with split ends.

Me: Ha! One day, I will miss you making me laugh. I will miss it a great deal.

———

Bedtime with my youngest is the most excruciating time of my day.

Me: You have got to get to bed! If dragging out bedtime was a class in school, you'd be the valedictorian.

Kate (pauses from running in circles in her pajamas): I don't know what that means. Let's discuss it.

Me: See. This is what I'm talking about.

———

Me: I'll let you pick out your cousin's birthday present.

Kate: Oh, that's easy. Boys are all about their balls.

Me: Excuse me.

Kate: You know, basketballs, baseballs, footballs. What were you thinking?

Me: That. Exactly that.

———

KATE'S SURPRISE BIRTHDAY PARTY

I collapse on the couch after an exhaustive day of teaching tweens. I check my eyelids for pinholes. Instantly, I hear the squeal of the air brakes on Claire and Kate's bus. I remain motionless like an animal in fear for its life. Which is accurate.

I feel the vibration of the garage door go up, hear them trying to ride the dog, and the rhythmic paired thumps of shoes being flung off into different parts of the universe. Kate spots me quivering on the couch and comes bounding toward me with entirely too much energy. I have long been a proponent of large hamster wheels for use in schools. It has not caught on.

My little first grader reaches into her bursting-at-the-seams backpack with one hand while slamming it to the carpet with the other hand. She is left gripping a wrinkled green paper like a magician who pulled a rabbit from a hat. She shoves it in my face while rambling on about a birthday party.

"I am sure you can go. Let me check the calendar," I say while rousing all the remaining energy in my body to sit up.

"The party is tonight. At Chuck E. Cheese."

"What! Why didn't you give me this invitation sooner?"

"I just got it. Today. And I REALLY want to go. Please."

I inspect the invitation. The party is for October 8. That's today. From six to eight. It is currently 4:38. It says RSVP Riya. Nothing more. No phone number. Nothing.

"What ethnicity is your friend Riya?" I ask.

"Oh, she's different from us, but the same," answers Kate, "and she is the nicest kid in my whole class. The nicest."

I've heard enough. I want Kate hanging out with the nicest kid. Hopefully some of it rubs off. I call The Better Half and tell her she is on her own for dinner. I'll drop Kate off at six at Chuck E. Cheese Kid Casino and then take Claire out to McDonald's across the street.

We rush over to Walmart to buy some worthless piece of plastic for the nicest girl in Kate's class. We rush back and throw it in a Christmas-themed gift bag because it's the only one we have. It's October, so close enough. And we're off to Chuck E. Cheese aka Catcha Disease.

We pull up to a building with a purple and red awning and a giant smiling rat overlooking everything. We walk through the doors at 6:01. Riya rushes up and hugs Kate. She is Indian. This is an Indian birthday party. Riya's mom is standing behind her and says, "This must be Kate." I'm shocked she knows my daughter on sight.

Riya is dressed like a princess. She is in a teal gown with her hair pulled back in a beautiful headband that matches her dress. Kate is in a T-shirt that makes it clear to everyone that she loves Darth Vader, leopard print leggings, and flip flops.

Riya's mom asks us to stay. All of us. Claire, my giant fourth grader compared to the first graders, is ecstatic to join the party. Her sister is less ecstatic about her staying. Kate looks at me with wide, expressive eyes that say, "Don't stay." I look back with squinty eyes that say, "I'm super cheap and this saves me a McDonald's trip." I pause. Does the mom really want us to stay? I don't want to be rude.

"Are you sure it is okay if we stay?" I ask the mom.

Her head bobs in a partial yes and partial no. I have no idea what to do. There is a good five seconds of awkward.

"Please, please stay. I have bought free play cards for all the kids. And food for everyone. Adults, too," she says.

She is gripping a handful of free play cards in her hand. For what seems to be three kids. I feel we should stay. No one came to this party but Ms. Leopard Pants and her big sister. I smile and nod.

Kate and Riya sprint off to play games. Claire takes off for a game where you spin a giant wheel like you are on *The Price is Right* and hope it lands on jackpot. There are a thousand other places it can stop. She will play this game the entire time. She will never win. The promised one-thousand-ticket jackpot is like the convertible rotating above the penny slots in Vegas.

I sit awkwardly with Riya's mom, she in a lavender dress and me in jeans and sweatshirt. The dad rolls in from his work in slacks and a dress shirt. They smile at me. I smile back. We all shake hands again. Everyone is so nice. I decide to stroll around a bit to see what goes on at a Chuck E. Cheese on a Tuesday night.

I go over to Claire and steal her free play card as she whines about not being able to play a game she'll never win. I hit the Pop-a-Shot game. I didn't get a college scholarship for my brains. I can straight up shoot a basketball. First time up I get seventy-two points. Record for the machine is seventy-eight. A fat kid with red hair and freckles watches me shoot my last few shots, crowding me like he's next. Whatever, kid. I swipe the card again and get a ball in my hands as the horn blares. I don't miss. Last ten seconds all shots count as three pointers. I nail every one. The fat kid stands there, mouth agape. I score one hundred points. Exactly. Tickets come pouring out of the machine. I am Wilt Chamberlain.

"I'll never get one hundred points," says the fat kid.

I'm an educator. I should encourage him to work hard. Tell him he can do it. But I'm off the clock.

"You're right," I answer while handing Claire an armful of tickets worth a Starburst in the Chuck E. Cheese economy.

I sit down in a booth, winded. A guy walks in. Early forties. No kids. Construction boots. Cement-stained jeans. Flannel button-up right out of a Nirvana video. Slips a free play card in the football game on the other side of Skee-Ball. It's called NFL Two Minute Drill. You get footballs and there are three openings. Biggest to smallest at the top. You get points each time a football goes through an opening. Random plastic receivers pop up and you are supposed to mow them down. A buzzer sounds, and this guy goes to work. He is throwing frozen ropes. Every pass a spiral and on target. First five go through the tiny top hole. Receiver pops up. Nailed without missing a beat. Straight Uncle Rico. Then he takes two steps back. Still nailing every throw. Two minutes up. The machine spits out a bundle of tickets. He swipes again. And again. Grabs his pile of tickets and walks over to the prize counter. He slides them over for three fun-size bags of Skittles. The lady doesn't even count the tickets. He's like a regular with a tab at the local watering hole.

I want to run after him. Tell him he is living a dream. Tell him he is my hero. That he is superior to half the quarterbacks in the NFL right now. Tell him I don't think I'd ever be able to throw a football like that. To which he'd respond, "You're right." Like a mist, he is gone.

"Have you seen the manager? I can't find the manager," says a lady with blond, stringy hair and tobacco-stained teeth. She's clearly invading my personal space.

"No," I answer, wondering why she thinks I would know the manager.

"That Skee-Ball machine shorted me ten tickets. Imma gettin' my tickets," she yells while walking away, dragging a toddler behind her. Ten tickets in this place are worth about one-tenth of a penny.

She forgets about the manager and heads for the beer tap. There is one tap sticking out of the wall behind the cash register like a spigot on a house. Just one kind of beer here. And the kind doesn't matter. I bet on a Saturday that thing is streaming beer like a fire hose.

At exactly 6:45, a Chuck E. Cheese employee, a lady in a purple polo shirt, starts rounding up Riya and her two guests. I feel bad that she has no one at her party. Suddenly, a hundred of her friends and relatives come pouring through the door. All of them Indian. There are kids running everywhere. Presents covering tables. People speaking other languages. It's crazy. I'm just a super tall white guy standing there. Every person makes a point to come over and shake my hand. They tell me how nice Kate is and thank me for bringing her. I consider immigrating to India. These are the nicest people I've ever met. Not even close to on time, but very nice. I see where Riya gets it.

The kids sit at a table that looks like a school lunch table. The parents group around the edges and in surrounding booths. There are twenty other empty tables around us. This is one party. On a Saturday, with twenty parties, this place must be a zoo. A Black Friday made up of tiny people with no functioning frontal cortex. So

Black Friday. Twenty tables and twenty parties. All day. No wonder the manager is MIA. He probably has PTSD.

Kate is seated right next to Riya. She's the only white kid at this party and she is oblivious to it. I love it. She just knows Riya is the nicest kid in her class, and that's all that matters. And it is.

A thirty-something lady in the purple polo shirt yells out to the table of kids.

"Who wants to see Chuck E. Cheese?"

They all scream noncoherent words. Music starts playing and someone in a giant rat costume wearing sneakers, jeans, and a rugby shirt comes strolling out. Chuck and purple polo lady do a coordinated dance to the music. Neither one of them is into it and you can tell. It is one of the saddest things I have ever seen. The person in the rat costume is not allowed to talk. If they could, I'm pretty sure they would say, "Do well in school kids. I didn't. That's why I am in a giant rat costume that is one thousand degrees and has never been laundered. The struggle is real."

Charles E. Cheese disappears, never to be seen again. Purple-polo woman puts on plastic gloves and starts handing out a piece of cheese pizza to each kid. Riya's dad tells me that he bought sandwiches for all the adults. A big platter of subs comes out and I pick the biggest one because I'm the biggest person here. I bite into my dinner. There is bread, lettuce, tomato, green pepper, and lettuce, and green pepper. They forgot my meat.

I glance at my phone. The Better Half has texted: "FYI, they may all be vegetarians." Too little, too late. I'm not sure whether to chew the veggie sub slowly or quickly. The Better Half wanted me to start eating healthier. No better time to start than the present. There's a good chance, though, I drive through Wendy's on the way home for a Baconator.

A big white cake comes out. Somehow Kate thinks this is her birthday, too, and helps blow out the candles. I step forward preparing to grab Kate in case Riya punches her. Good thing Riya's the nicest girl in the class. They hug and smile. There are fifty perfectly wrapped presents on the table behind them. And one Christmas gift bag. I consider taking the tag off, but they'd know it was us. Nothing else we've done has fit in tonight. Purple-polo takes the cake into the back to be cut and the kitchen door flies open. I see a bunch of tattoos and failed rap careers working back there.

Purple-polo reappears and starts handing out pieces of cake from a tray. I realize I have a real problem. I'm hoping Kate doesn't somehow use a Jedi mind trick to steal the cake from all the other kids. Although everyone is so nice, they'd probably just give her their cake. Still, I can't have her puking in my car on the way home.

The hostess runs out of cake when she gets to Claire. Much-older Claire looks like she's going to cry because she's not getting cake at a first-grade birthday party she wasn't invited to. Riya's dad asks me if I have seen the manager. Why does everyone think I know the manager? He's probably cowering in the bathroom. That's what I would do.

He goes off in search of missing white birthday cake for the giant white girl. But before leaving, he apologizes profusely ... for the cake and that there were supposed to be more subs for the adults. I tell him I'm good with my one lettuce and green pepper extravaganza. "Thanks."

I gather my girls to let them know that we've been here longer than everyone else and the party technically ended fifteen minutes ago. They whine, but I drag them to a machine called the "Ticket Muncher" where they gleefully feed hundreds of prize tickets into it while it makes chewing sounds as it grinds up the tickets. You buy free play cards to get tickets to put in a machine that munches them up and gives you a ticket total that you then take to a glass case of cool prizes. But your total of munched tickets may not be enough to afford any of them. A genius business model.

Claire decides to save her four hundred twenty-seven tickets for a promised future Chuck E. Cheese visit that I am lying about. Kate decides to spend every ticket and uses a ridiculous amount of time looking into the glass case debating between a blow-up plastic hand to slap her sister with or six Tootsie Rolls. She picks slapping her sister all the way home over her sweet tooth. I allow it since the Tootsie Rolls combined with the extra cake she undoubtedly snagged from the nicest people in the world would make her puke. We pile back in my SUV for the ride home. It's a school night. Already too late for baths. We will have to go to school tomorrow with the Chuck E. stank, which seems to be a combination of cheap pizza and feet.

"See, Dad, I told you," says Kate while slapping her sister with her new toy. "Riya is the nicest."

"She is. They were about the nicest people I have ever met."

"And I got some extra cake," she whispers while the car gets ominously silent.

"If I have to stay up all night cleaning this car, I might die," I answer, half-joking.

"I'll miss you, Dad."

4
CLAIRE SAVES DAD

AND SO IT BEGINS

It was a typical pregnancy. Until it wasn't. It was a Sunday morning. We were getting ready for church. The Better Half started "spotting." I needed her to explain what that meant. We rushed to the hospital. We didn't know much about having babies, as this was our first, but we knew this one couldn't yet make it outside of Mommy. It was too soon in the pregnancy for a baby to arrive.

As we sat in the OB/GYN wing of the hospital waiting room, The Better Half tapped her fingers on my knee. She was worried. Me, not so much. She had bonded to the little one growing inside of her. Me, not so much.

A nurse led us back to a row of three tiny exam rooms separated by curtains. She instructed The Better Half to remove her pants and underwear. She handed her what looked like a napkin. I wasn't sure whether it was for modesty or to wipe up some leftover crumbs from breakfast. Then she asked a hundred questions, including: "Did we just finish having sex?" No. It's Sunday morning, you heathen. We should be in church right now.

Two guys in scrubs and white coats strolled in. Finally, the doctors. Same hundred questions. No, we did not just finish having sex. Couldn't someone talk to the nurse? I looked a little more closely at the badge one was wearing. Interns doing rounds. Crap. These were people who wanted to be doctors but were probably not much interested in babies. The life of my unborn child was in the hands of two future dermatologists. Wonderful.

One of them nervously pulled out a foot-long wand with a sphere on the end about the size of a ping pong ball. Made me glad I wasn't the one sitting on an exam table with my pants off, wearing a napkin. He sent the other intern to the "condom room" to get a condom to put over the ping pong ball.

I watched him leave, and my eyes got wide. There's a condom room here? I pictured a room lined with boxes of condoms. Geez, these neonatal doctors were serious about not knocking up some nurse. Guess they had seen enough babies. Kind of how the guy working at the chocolate factory never wanted a candy bar.

The wannabe doctor came back to report that the condom room was locked, and they didn't have the key. They both looked sad and not concerned about the worried patient spread-eagle in front of them wearing a napkin. Instead, they worried they'd not get to check this procedure off their monthly checklist. I secretly wished proctology rounds on them next.

The one who looked like MacGyver got a MacGyver idea. He grabbed a latex glove and forced the thumb over the probe while his buddy smiled. They both nodded at each other, confirming their brilliance.

In went the gloved probe, down went the lights. They whispered to each other. They had a look of concern, which caused my wife to panic. They called me back to the glowing screen.

"There may be a tear in the placenta. See that dark line? I don't need to tell you that, at twenty-three weeks, we are on the edge of viability," MacGyver said in a somber tone.

"Can you tell us the sex of the baby?" I asked while squinting at some kind of Rorschach ink blot on a black and white screen.

He moved the wand like he was stirring coffee and examined the screen.

"Nope. I can't tell."

I now had zero confidence in these two clowns.

"Strange. The tear seems to move," he said.

He squinted while the screen made his face glow in the darkened room. The other one left the room to get the attending physician. He squeezed my shoulder as he walked out. There's nothing like false comfort from some guy happy to get a box checked off his procedure list.

A lady with high heels and frazzled red hair strolled in. Finally, a real doctor. She looked at the screen for two seconds and then down at my wife. She glared at the wannabe doctors.

"The tear you think you see is the seam on the end of the latex glove you're using to cover the probe. That's why it moves. Always keep the key to the condom room on you."

This last part was said as more of a warning against reproducing than hospital protocol. I smiled at them. Sorry fellows, sometimes you're the pigeon; sometimes you're the statue. They slumped out.

I asked about the sex of the baby. She couldn't tell either. She told us to follow up with our regular OB the next day. Follow up on what? The seam of a latex glove?

At the office of our regular OB, he also asked whether we'd had sex. It was a Monday. In the middle of the day. Every pregnant couple in the world must have been having a lot more sex than we were.

"Can you tell us if it's a boy or girl?"

He glanced at the ultrasound screen for a few seconds. "It's a girl." He gave The Better Half a stern look. "One more problem and you are going on bedrest in the hospital. Until then, bedrest at your house."

I shuddered. Bedrest was not something that came naturally to The Better Half. There were rumors that she once took a nap in 1995. Rumors. This was one time in our marriage when I really did wish I could bear her burden. I could bedrest like it was a job. Like a hibernating grizzly bear. I was born for this.

I went out and bought a wooden bed tray with little folding legs. I got her all set up to lie on the couch all day long. I looked wistfully at her as I headed to work. "Stay," I said as though commanding an untrained puppy.

I got home from work, and she had the look of a kid with chocolate all over his face. Laundry was folded. Dishwasher was empty. Not a crumb on the kitchen floor.

"How was the bedrest?"

"Good," she lied.

She spotted again. We both knew what that meant. We were sixteen weeks from the due date ... four months of living in the hospital. We packed the bags, and she moved into a hospital corner room. Every day was the same. Go to work at 6:30 a.m. Come home at 3:15 p.m. Let the dog out. Drive to the hospital. Stay until I got drowsy. Come home. Start over. It was monotonous. It was boring. Depressing. I hated going to the hospital, but like all living things, I adapted.

In my down time, I started exploring. The hospital was a city unto itself. There were two high-rise towers. Doors to nowhere, bathrooms everywhere, carts of food that sat out for hours. And no one paid any attention to me. If I became homeless, I was not living on the street. I was living here.

In this weird place, the highest members of society were in constant contact with the lowest. The doctors and nurses became numb to people. I didn't even register to them ... I was just some guy walking the halls at night. I got to know the chain smokers freezing their butts off, gowns flapping while standing in front of the hospital, still attached to IV drips and leaning on the "No Smoking" signs. I always got a high five from the lady who emptied the trash cans at midnight.

My best friend was Charles. I didn't know his name, but he looked like a Charles to me. Charles was the big black guy who made me my food in the hospital cafeteria. The grilled cheese and homemade potato chips for $3.27 was the best deal in the joint. I started chatting with Charles every day, and he started giving me twice as many chips as everyone else.

Back home, my water heater broke. So, cold showers, which felt appropriate for my mood. I let our seventy-pound goldendoodle sleep with me. She snored like my pregnant wife, and her legs were only slightly more hairy. Although when a dog gets restless leg syndrome, it's twice as bad.

One Saturday, I got bold and brought our dog to the hospital. I just walked in the front door like I was supposed to be bringing in a giant dog. No one said a word. Until I got on the elevator. The door closed, and a fat lady talking on her phone yelled to the person she was talking to: "Oh my God! There's a dog in here! I think it's going to attack me!"

I just looked at her and said, "What's she going to do, lick you to death?" The dog and I got off at the next floor and took the stairs. What had the world come to if a guy couldn't walk his giant dog around a hospital without an explanation?

The depressing life that was slowly killing me was nothing compared to what The Better Half was going through. Lying in a bed all day, wires attached all over her belly. Hospital food instead of delicious grilled cheese made by Charles. Steroid shots in the hip. I had it easy compared to her.

Six weeks into this nightmare, I decided I needed a hot shower. I was a bit of a hermit crab before getting married, and I still knew the entry code to one of the houses I had occupied then. No one was home. Perfect. Halfway through my shower, I heard my old roomie's wife, Sheri, outside the bathroom door. "You better get to the hospital," she said in a distinct, you're-having-a-baby tone. Oh boy.

I rushed to the hospital. I shook the hand of each of the guys who were outside smoking while freezing their butts off in hospital gowns. Ironically, I had no cigars to pass out. I waved at Charles while running by the cafeteria. "I think we're having a baby, Charles." He looked at me like: "Who the heck is Charles?"

I bounded into the corner room. The Better Half had set up quite a little nest. It looked like a homeless person had claimed ten square feet under a bridge. But the nest was empty; there was no Better Half. I started to freak out. Where was my wife? A nurse stuck her head in and said she'd "call around" and try to find her. How do you lose a pregnant lady on bedrest?

She returned with my wife's new room number and a little metal cart. It looked like one of those toy shopping carts kids play with.

"This room needs to be cleaned out. Right now. Someone else is scheduled in here."

What was this place, a motel that charged by the hour? My wife might have been in labor right then! And she had so much crap in there. I moved seven times when I was single, every time with less stuff than what filled this hospital room.

My buddy's wife, Sheri, showed up. She grabbed the metal cart and my car keys. Little angel wings sprouted from her back.

"Go to your wife. I got this," she said.

It was January 21. We were ten weeks early. Ten weeks! Our due date was April 1. April Fools! We were going to have a baby instead on Martin Luther King Jr. Day.

I joined my wife in a much smaller room. No one was telling us anything. I heard whispers of leaked water. Braxton Hicks. A giant exercise ball sat in the corner. I had no idea what was going on. The hospital had given us a video to watch about having a baby. But like a Netflix series we didn't really want to watch, we had put it off. We thought we had plenty of time. And now the only things I knew about having a baby were what I'd seen on TV.

Finally, an older nurse came on duty. She looked like she may have been a linebacker for the Chicago Bears in another life.

"I bet you have this baby at 2 a.m.," she stated with confidence.

"We're having her tonight?"

"Why do you think you're in labor and delivery?"

Duh. I didn't have the guts to tell her we knew nothing about having a baby. Nothing. I really wanted to ask what they did with that exercise ball. And if I could play with it. And who was Braxton Hicks? But I was happy with the prediction of birth four hours from now.

The nurse said that when the pain got to a 7, The Better Half could have an epidural.

"What would you say your pain is now?" she leadingly asked.

"I'm at a 6.5," answered The Better Half confidently. The linebacker walked out.

"You can't round up? Seriously!" I said, glaring at her. This was one time her perfectionism was going to cost her. Dearly.

I ran out in the hallway and told linebacker that we just had a little pain spike. Exactly a point five. She got the epidural for us.

We still hadn't seen a doctor. Just the linebacker nurse. The Better Half said she felt contractions despite the epidural. Linebacker checked her "down there" and said that she was at a 4. I had no idea what that meant, but she smiled like she was still proud of her 2 a.m. prediction. Good enough for me. She tucked in The Better Half and told her to take a nap.

I ran down to get some grilled cheese from Charles. He wasn't working, so I got some soup. Back in the room, I was innocently eating my soup when linebacker decided to check her "down there" again. Better Half was wearing some giant diaper contraption. I just ate my soup.

Linebacker started huffing and puffing. She ran to the door and screamed out in the hallway, "Ten Plus!" I had no idea what this meant. But suddenly, the over/under on the 2 a.m. prediction seemed like a long shot. Several people came in, grabbed the bed, and we were rolling down the hallway into an even smaller room. I really wanted to bring the giant exercise ball.

Our OB, an older guy with glasses, stuck his bald head into the room. He had come from a party, and he was dressed in a suit. He pulled the curtain that separated the rooms close to his body like he was dressed inappropriately or in the shower.

"Let me get some jammies on and we'll have a baby."

A man rolled a long skinny table down near the feet of The Better Half. It was covered in what looked like little rolled up sleeping bags. He carefully unrolled each one. A saw. Knives. A sickle. All shiny stainless steel. The Better Half couldn't see any of this. I gulped hard.

"How are you doing?" The Better Half asked me.

"Fine," I lied, not wanting to tell her they were planning on killing her.

"Would you like to use the mirrors?" asked a nurse. For the first time, I saw that there were mirrors strategically placed into the ceiling with bright lights surrounding them. The place was like a fun house of horrors. Who watched themselves give birth? I wasn't sure I wanted to watch. There was a pause. In my mind, I was thinking, "Don't use the mirrors. Don't use the mirrors. You will be watching them murder you."

"No thanks," answered The Better Half.

Whew.

Suddenly, five people silently filed into the tiny room. They were shoulder to shoulder. I looked around. What was going on? Was this some kind of circus show? Were we having an alien baby?

Our OB motioned for me to leave the head section of my wife and to come join him. I gave her a shoulder squeeze and nervously craned my neck next to his head.

"The baby's crowning," he said.

I glanced down and smiled back at him. In my mind, I was absolutely freaking out. Freaking the heck out. There was a little ball of black hair, smaller than a ping pong ball, sticking out. That was the baby's head! Girl or boy? Regardless, this kid was going to be the size of a Troll Doll with the hair to match. Maybe she was going to wear Barbie clothes and sit in the palm of my hand. Maybe Baby Tom Thumb was about to be born.

The Better Half groaned in pain. I looked over at the stainless-steel torture tools. I vehemently encouraged her to push for all she was worth. She didn't even know that they were prepared to kill her. And how hard could it be to push out a Troll Doll?

Then bloop. A giant, normal human head popped out. It was super pointy at the end, like a sharpened pencil. They probably explained that in the video we never watched. One more big push and out came a girl, Claire Marie, into the world.

Everyone started congratulating The Better Half. The baby was a little over three pounds. I felt confident I'd had larger bowel movements, and no one congratulated me. I squeezed a "Great Job" in there nonetheless.

Suddenly, the five silent people sprang into action. Identification bands were attached to baby Claire. A giant plastic aquarium was rolled into the room. Tubes were everywhere, cylinders of air started pumping, and Claire got a little striped stocking cap on her pointy head.

The Better Half reached in a porthole on the side of the aquarium and petted her daughter one time before she was rolled away. Both of them were crying. The Better Half told me to go with Claire.

Here was the thing; I didn't really care about Claire. I cared about my wife. I thought getting a baby was going to be like getting a puppy. Instead, I got a goldfish in a bowl.

The next six weeks mirrored the last. Woke up. Came to the hospital every day. Spent it with a baby that didn't know I existed. Went home late at night. I was on paternity leave. Which resembled getting a new job at an aquarium store that only had one fish.

One day, we went to Claire's room and she was gone. This hospital had a habit of losing people. A nurse led us to a nursery full of preemie babies. It was silent except for the beeps of machines.

"Why is it so quiet?" I whispered.

"Preemies never cry. They think they are still in the womb," answered the nurse.

The next day, one of the boys got circumcised. He cried. All day. Couldn't say I blamed him.

I'm pretty sure the dog was pissed that The Better Half was back home, and she had to return to sleeping on the floor. To me, it was just someone else who snored and generally had hairy legs.

I feel shameful now admitting this, but I didn't really care for my new aquarium pet. She reminded me of the Pet Rock craze from the 1970s. People doting on something that didn't even know they were there. Or care. She just lived in a climate-controlled, clear bin and passively ate from a tube inserted in her nose.

Then we got to bring her home. Goody. After six weeks in the hospital. Coming home a month before she was supposed to be born. More of this little baby lying around bundled up like a tiny burrito. Except now she cried. A lot.

I went back to work in a sleep-deprived, depressed, daze. A tiny hand grenade had been tossed into my life, my marriage, my bed. This was not the puppy I had been promised.

A dark sadness overtook my life. I had dealt before with what Winston Churchill called "The Black Dog." But never like this. This was Godzilla and I was Tokyo.

I started to die inside. I never laughed. I was perpetually solemn and sad. Driving home, alone, I reached a breaking point. I wanted out. This was not what I had signed up for. I always thought guys who left their kids and marriages were horrible excuses for human beings. Gaining empathy is never fun.

Three pounds and eight ounces of baby was all it took to ruin my happy little life.

Later that night, I was cooking meat loaf. As I was taking it out, it flipped over in the oven and started scorching. Smoke poured out. I just started screaming in anger.

I grabbed at the drawer next to the stove to get another oven mitt in hopes of retrieving my meatloaf. A metal spatula had jammed itself in the drawer. I pulled hard on the drawer handle. The spatula said, "Not today."

Still screaming, I went all Incredible Hulk on that drawer. Ripped it right out of the cabinet, breaking it in half. I slammed the offending spatula to the ground and started beating it with another spatula in a kind of forced spatula-on-spatula retribution. I was still screaming. At spatulas.

I turned around, red faced, to see The Better Half gripping baby Claire in her arms. She looked at me in fear. This wasn't me. Who had I become? The baby had done this to me.

I needed to leave. The house. The marriage. And above all that baby.

I needed to do anything to lift the sadness that darkened my life. I was drowning. And Claire was the weight pulling me down. I couldn't even see the light of the surface anymore. I knew my next breath would kill me. As any drowning person does, I thrashed around. Violently. I needed to break free. But it was too dark. Too deep.

I needed a reason to live. A reason to exist. Someone to reach through the storm, waves, and water. But there was no one.

I was suffocating. All by myself.

No one would save me now.

———————

Just read baby Claire the book *Goodnight Moon*. The synopsis on the back is longer than the book. That's like the preview being longer than the movie. I read the synopsis to her as well, just to feel like I got more "book value."

———————

The Better Half is nuts. She babyproofed the whole house for a baby who can't roll over. In the kitchen, I can't get the silverware drawer open. These child-proof latches are a Rubik's Cube. I'm just going to eat this pudding cup with my hands and call it a day.

———————

Took a baby Trick or Treating. People give a baby twice the candy they give a full-size kid. A baby can't even eat the candy they are giving her. But her dad can.

———————

Yesterday, the baby loved these creamed peas. Today, she hates them. This makes no sense. It's as if the cow looked up at the farmer and said, "Today, this hay tastes like crap," then spit it all over the kitchen floor.

Set the baby down in front of the Christmas tree. She broke a glass bulb and screamed. The dog came running. I got both of them behind the baby gate. While I was cleaning up every sliver of glass, the baby pried two keys off the laptop keyboard and ate one. If she doesn't poop out a RETURN key, all communication from that computer will become a run-on sentence.

Took Claire for a one-year checkup at the pediatrician. She fell in the 90th percentile in height but in the 10th percentile for weight. The Better Half is worried. I'm not. We're growing a supermodel.

The in-laws are visiting. As dinner started, Claire insisted on showing off her new hangnail. Our meal began with everyone getting flicked off by a two-year-old. Classy.

Claire has taught me that a two-year-old has two speeds: smile and sprint.

Every morning, I pack Claire into her car seat to drive her to the sitter. Her puffy coat leaves her arms perpetually extended outward. We ride in silence through the dark. Until seventeen minutes in, when we pass a pasture full of cows chewing cud. On cue, I hear her one morning word: "Moo."

I taught Claire to blow on her food if it is hot. She wanted to go down the slide at the park. It was a sunny day. I told her the slide would burn her. The sun made it hot. She squatted down and started blowing on it.

I have Claire convinced that I am a superhero with only one weakness: my ears. Because she was a preemie, we had an evaluator come to our house from the school district. Claire was sitting on my lap while the serious lady with a PhD was asking her some questions. Claire cupped her hands to my face and said, "Time to get your ear." And playfully bit my ear. The lady with the PhD was probably thinking, *I hope they homeschool*.

THE GAME

Jim: Hello, parenting fans, and welcome to this morning's contest. Today, we will see Claire, age 3 (or 41 months as her mother would say), take on Dad, age 38 (or 456 months as his mother might say). Claire is 3 ft. 2 inches tall and just a shade over thirty pounds. Dad is 6 ft. 8 inches tall and well over two hundred and forty pounds. Looks like a mismatch, doesn't it, Carl?

Carl: You can say that again. After twenty straight wins, "the little terror" is a heavy favorite. Vegas has Dad throwing in the towel in less than an hour. Jim, you've raised two kids. What can Dad do different to give himself a chance?

Jim: He has to keep Claire guessing. Get her on the defensive. Lie. Feed her junk food. And hope she runs out of energy before he does. He needs caffeine, and he has to make sure she avoids it. Remember the game where she guzzled half a can of leftover Mountain Dew before nap time? Now that was a slaughter. This is destined to be a race to the afternoon nap. That's if she takes one.

Carl: Looks like we are about to kick this game off. Claire just opened the door to her dad's room. I have 6:17 a.m. on the game/alarm clock. Fans, here we go. She circles his bed like a shark. Look at her staring him down; those eyes, they are so black, devoid of empathy. Now she unexpectedly prances back out, her naturally mulleted blonde head barely visible over the mattress. She returns carrying something purple and cone-shaped. Jim, what is that?

Jim: An instrument of torture if there ever was one: a cheerleader megaphone. A gift from her aunt, it falls into the same category as her ball-popping lawnmower that has no batteries to remove and her one-thousand-piece plastic tea set. Gifts kids love and parents despise. She's placing it next to Dad's ear. Wow! I never heard the phrase "I have to go potty" as a pterodactyl screech.

Carl: Claire has taken a commanding early lead. Dad stumbles out of bed, grasping for clothes and giving no care to whether items are clean or dirty, matching or a fashion nightmare. This is the type of situation that can quickly devolve into a dad in jean shorts, dress socks, and sandals. His eyes bloodshot, hair matted, teeth yellow and hamster-like. Not the strong start Dad was hoping for.

Jim: Dad stumbles down the hallway. Ouch, just stepped on a metal toy car with his left foot and a plastic tea cup with his right. Time for the classic "hop and howl." Claire screeches with laughter. It's almost too easy for her as she toys with him. Hasn't Claire been going to the bathroom alone recently?

Carl: That's right, Jim. Looks like she just tricked Dad into walking through the classic toy minefield. Well played, little lady. She climbs up on the toilet, without any help, and perches on the seat like a gymnast on a pommel horse. Claire grunts, followed by some splashes. She whispers something about kids and a daddy.

Jim: I believe she is telling her dad that her first two small bowel movements are babies in the pool, and now she has a big daddy coming. Nice touch using fecal matter to refer to Daddy.

Carl: Time to move to Claire's home court, her bedroom. This is where she is undefeated. Looks like Dad has tried to gain an advantage by laying out her outfit the night before. He's got the pants on, and now for the turtleneck. He's forcing it over her head, she wiggles, I see a tuft of blonde hair ... he got it! Big score by Dad. But he's looking around. Where are the socks? He forgot to lay out socks! Dad is forced to turn his back on her to get the socks out of the top drawer and ...

Jim: Just that quick, she is naked again. She is so fast, a very impressive athlete. The defeated look on Dad's face really tells the story. He has to start all over; it's like dressing cooked spaghetti. He exhales and cedes the point to Claire. She will be dressing herself. Looks like she will be wearing last year's Halloween costume all day.

Carl: Next, we are headed downstairs for breakfast. Dad is asking if she wants cereal or a frozen waffle. Claire wants mac and cheese. She is stomping her foot while speaking, like a bull pawing the ground before a charge.

Jim: Looks like Dad is already giving up. He's boiling water and pouring a mixing bowl of Lucky Charms for himself. He slides a steaming bowl of mac and cheese across the table to Claire like a hopeless bartender. Claire says she spilled some cheese. Dad is looking, finding nothing. Claire excuses herself to go potty again, and a trail of cheese is left across the kitchen floor.

Carl: Brilliant, hiding the cheese on the heel of her left foot. Her dexterity is amazing.

Jim: Now Dad is wrestling her into that straitjacket of a car seat. You get the feeling that, if he can get her buckled in, he might just leave her there all day. A trip to story time at the library. It's half an hour, and it's free. A potential two-point conversion for Dad.

Carl: Dad starts the car. He forgot to change the radio channel from the last time he drove alone. Claire is singing something about "Sexy Time." If Coach Mom hears Claire singing this song, she is going to intentionally foul Dad. Dad is reaching into his pocket and offering a "deal" for some candy. She accepts. Good recovery by Dad, but there is also the chance that Claire is just throwing a pump fake his way.

Jim: We arrive at the library. Story time just started, so let's take a minute for our library stat break down:

18-1 Moms to Dads at story time.

15-3 Moms doing hand motions to the songs to kids doing the hand motions.

7-1 Moms dressed up because "they're still hot" to moms that actually are.

1-17 Moms who clearly do not believe in spanking to moms who wish she did.

Carl: Dad is distracted by that one hot mom, and that is all the opportunity Claire needs. She is sprinting around the story circle, hitting other kids on the head yelling "Duck" despite the fact they are not playing Duck, Duck, Goose. This could be a very embarrassing moment for Dad.

Jim: Looks like Dad is getting off the hook on this one. All the moms are just laughing as he chases Claire around. This time, being a male pays off. The female-dominated group appreciates him just showing up and probably secretly wishes their male counterparts would do the same. Looked like Claire was going to put the game away, but Dad keeps hanging around. Time for Dad to carry a screaming Claire surfboard-style to the car and head for home.

Carl: Back on her home turf, Claire demands mac and cheese for lunch. She is turning on the water works. Dad reheats breakfast and begrudgingly shoves a plate over to her. Defeated. He thought he had a chance today. Look at him. He's not even eating, just burying his face in his hands and praying a child can develop normally eating only one type of food.

Jim: He trudges upstairs carrying an exhausted Claire to her room for her nap. He tucks her in bed. She whispers in his ear, asking for a hug. He leans over and hugs her and then pulls back. Little Claire asks for "just one more." Dad smiles and hugs again. He turns to leave. Claire asks for "just one more hug."

Carl: This is a classic stall technique. She is just running some time off the clock on another convincing victory. Here comes another request for a hug. Wait a minute. Jim, are you seeing this?

Jim: I cannot believe this! She is really hugging him. Now she is saying he is "the best dad ever." And "they are a team." She's joining his team! Tears are forming at the edges of Dad's eyes. What a rally by Dad. And what is Claire doing? Here comes another hug! Her huge lead is evaporating.

Carl: We have never seen a comeback like this in the sport of child rearing. At the buzzer ... DAD WINS! DAD WINS!

I have to get Claire potty trained before this next baby comes. I cannot mentally or financially afford to have double diapers going on in this house. Every time she pees in the potty, she gets an M&M, and every time she poops in the potty, she gets a sucker. I'll have her potty trained by the end of the week. Her teeth will be rotting out, but I won't have to deal with her diapers. Deal.

The M&M and sucker training is going great. Leading to this bathroom door conversation:

Claire: Daddy, open door. I come in.
Me: Not now. I'm going to the bathroom. Please stay out.
Claire: You getting sucker?
Me: Oh yeah. Definitely a sucker. A big sucker.

When you give your kid a lollipop every time they poop on the potty, they are going to yell for a sucker while pooping. Since a two-year-old can't say their "S's" very well, and it comes out as an "F," it sounds like they are yelling the F-bomb. I found this out today while standing next to Claire in a stall in a grocery store bathroom. She kept yelling it louder and louder. I'd like to apologize to the patrons of the Main Street grocery store. Note to self: Keep suckers on person at all times.

Claire (praying): God, thank you for my food ... and thank you for my food ... and thank you for my food ... and thank you for my food ...

Me: Okay, you have thanked God for your food like seven times.

Claire: I know. I ate a lot of different stuff today.

Claire carefully inspects the grill of my car.

Claire: There are A LOT of dead bugs on here.

Me: Those are bugs who did not hold their daddy's hand when crossing the street. Learn from their sacrifice.

A conversation screamed through a locked bathroom door with a shower running.

Claire (furiously jiggling the door handle): Why is this door locked? I want to come in and talk to you. Tell you about my day.

Me: I'm taking a shower. You need to stay out.

Claire: But I thought we were a TEAM!

Me: We are. It's just that you can't see boys naked. It's a rule. I'm so sorry.

Claire: I don't think Mom is going to like this new rule.

Me: She might like it more than you think.

Once again, the locked bathroom door is jiggling.

Claire: Let me in! I have to go potty!

Me: There are two other bathrooms in this house. Go find one. I am taking a shower.

Claire: But I like your bathroom. C'mon. I wanna sit on the potty and tell you about my day!

Me: Not going to happen. Sorry, honey.

Claire: I feel like our team is falling down.

———————

Dear Claire,

Before you were born, I used to have this thing called free time. I watched scary movies. In some of these movies, like *The Others*, *Children of the Corn*, *The Ring*, and *Pet Cemetery*, there were kids that were freaky scary. When I roll over at 2:42 in the morning and you are standing next to my bed and staring me in the face, it really terrifies me. Don't do that.

Dad

———————

Claire: Excuse me, Dad. I just burped.

Me: You are excused.

Claire: Yeah, it was just my tummy saying it would like to get out and play.

Tried to sleep in this morning. Ineffective as usual. Claire crawled into bed to cuddle.

Claire: Hello, teammate. I like to attach myself to your back in the morning. I'm like a leech.

Me: I think that is a fair description.

Claire: You know how to get rid of me? Get the leech off you?

Me: I'd like to know.

Claire: Tickling. Lots of tickling.

Claire's Prayer tonight:

Dear God,

    Thank you for everything. Thank you for my family. Thank you for me not coloring on the wall with crayon. Yet.

Amen

Claire: Mom! Baby needs you!

Me: I'm right here. I can help her. A daddy can help too.

Claire: She wants to eat a boob.

Me: Mom! Baby needs you!

Today, Claire slurped down a bowl of Cheerios for breakfast in record time, which led to this conversation:

Claire: One more, please.

Me: Wow, you are hungry. One more bowl coming right up.

Claire: No. One more Cheerio.

Me: Seriously.

Claire: Yes, my tummy is almost full. Just one Cheerio short.

———————

Claire: If something ever happens to Mom, I'm going to take her place in our house. 'Cause we are a team, Dad. Me and you.

Me: Nothing is ever going to happen to Mom. And you couldn't do laundry. And what about baby Kate?

Claire: Ummmm … The team is really just me and you. Kate can live with some other family. She'll be happy. I'm not sure she likes us that much anyway. But me and you, we cannot be separated.

———————

Claire: Dad, you are going to be the first one in our family to die.

Me: Probably. I'm the oldest.

Claire: Yeah, you are REALLY old.

Me: Why do you think I'm really old?

Claire: Well, things start small and grow bigger. Like trees. Just look around. You're bigger than everyone else. So, you are really old. I'll miss you, Dad.

Me: Thanks.

Me: Hey, Claire, you look like you are thinking about something.

Claire: I was thinking my last poop had a lot of corn in it. What are you thinking, Daddy?

Me: Thinking I will never again ask a four-year-old what she is thinking.

Claire: Did you know water goes around in a motorcycle?

Me: What?

Claire: You know, the sun makes vaperation. The motorcycle.

Me: Are you trying to say water cycle?

Claire: I'm pretty sure it's motorcycle.

Me: I'm a science teacher. It's water cycle.

Claire: No. At my school, we learned motorcycle. Water goes around in a motorcycle.

Today, we had a birthday party for Kate. Why we have a birthday party for a one-year-old, I will never know.

CLAIRE'S OUTFIT:

Pink Shirt: Festive

Black Leggings: Fashionable

Green and Red Christmas Socks: It is November 9, close enough.

And Under It All … A Bathing Suit.

Because, according to Claire, "You never know when you might end up swimming."

Words to live by.

Claire: What is today?

Me: Friday.

Claire: Is that the day it snows?

Me: It doesn't snow on just one particular day of the week.

Claire: It doesn't?

Me: Just kidding. Tuesday. It only snows on Tuesday. Don't tell Mom you know that.

Claire: You really need to get some princess shoes like me. They are so cool.

Me: As much as I would love some bejeweled, purple, high-heeled princess shoes, they simply do not make them in my size.

Claire: I guess there are good and bad things about being so big.

Me: Oh yeah, name a good thing.

Claire: I don't see anyone giving you a spanking. Ever.

Me: Good point.

Claire: What is that ouchie on your face?

Me: It's a zit. You will learn about them soon enough.

Claire: Would you like one of my Hello Kitty Band-Aids to put on it?

Me: No thanks.

Claire: Okay, but a Hello Kitty Band-Aid can fix about anything. Heals it good.

Me: I'll keep that in mind.

Me: This summer we can go to the beach and make sand castles.

Claire: I think I'll make pizza castles.

Claire spent the night with her aunt and uncle. I called to talk to her.

Me: Hi, Claire. What are you doing?

Claire: I'm riding in a car. We just got pizza. Can you smell it?

Me: No. I am on a phone.

Claire: Try sniffing real hard.

I took our goldendoodle to the vet. Claire really wanted to come. She then insisted on having the dog ride right next to her car seat. I could hear her whisper to the dog.

"You're gonna get some shots, and they're gonna hurt. But I'll hold your paw, and you try and think of something happy like chasing bunnies."

Claire (digging in her empty pockets): Dad, I got a piece of candy in here that I saved for you. Ummm … It must have died.

Me: You sure you didn't eat it?

Claire: I'm sure. It died. You know, things die and then they just disappear.

Me: A lot of your Halloween candy might die tonight after you go to bed.

Claire got a digital camera that is made for kids. She was horrible at it. Took over one hundred pictures of who knows what. Yesterday, she finally figured it out. She took three perfectly focused pictures of The Better Half getting out of the shower. We got a little Annie Leibovitz on our hands here. In each picture, you can almost hear her mom yelling "No!" with her hands up and Claire laughing.

Claire: Do you remember when I got this amazing medal I have around my neck?

Me: Yes. You were developmentally delayed, so we got you into a special gymnastics class. They had a ceremony with a platform. You were the only kid to get their medal and then fall off the platform.

Claire: I still have the medal. And now I am a wonderful gymnast! Claire turns and runs into a closed door, hits her head, and falls down.

Me: Claire, you did a great job of cleaning your plate for dinner. Do you want more of anything else?

Claire: No. I don't want anything else. But there is a square hole in my tummy.

Me: I'm picking up what you're laying down, Ms. Brownie.

Claire: Okay everyone, raise your hand if you want to play a game.

Me: I'm the only one here.

Claire: I'm still looking for that hand.

(I raise my hand.)

Claire: I see that volunteer. Good. This game has twelve steps.

Me: What is this game?

Claire: I don't know. Never played it before. Step one is think of a name.

———————

In ancient times, pirates would abandon people on a desert island chained to a dead body. The idea was the condemned person would be unable to escape the fact that the attached body was their fate as well. I am in a similar situation. Home all day with a vomitous Claire, who has declared her only plan for the day is "cuddle with Daddy." I will adjust my menu accordingly.

———————

Claire: Dad, me and you are a team. We need a name for our team.

Me: Any ideas?

Claire: Yeah. We'll be The Stinkers. Not stinkers like a toot. Like trouble stinkers. Cause Mom is always saying, "What are you two stinkers up to?"

———————

Car Seat Conversation

Me: Claire, a little bird told me you got to be the Happy Helper at preschool today. Tell me about that.

Claire: What? You have a little bird that tells you stuff?

Me: It's just an expression. Tell me about being the Happy Helper.

Claire: Is this bird like a puppet or like a real bird that flies around outside and talks?

Me: It's just a bird that tells me everything you do. Don't let it bother you.

There is a man with a white beard who works at the grocery store. There is a man with a white beard who plays the organ at church. Claire believes these men are one in the same. They are Santa. Leading to this conversation:

Claire: Santa did a good job playing the organ at church. But why does he work at the grocery store?

Me: He has to keep an eye on you. Plus, this economy has been hard on everyone. Even Santa needed to pick up some extra cash.

Claire: What is a conomy? Why is it hard on people?

Me: Don't concern yourself with that. Be good at church and at the store. And don't ask for too much at Christmas.

Car Seat Conversation:

Claire: Dad, I was thinking about something.

Me: What were you thinking?

Claire: Pooping is kinda like your bum getting sick and throwing up.

Me: No. It's completely different. Let's play the quiet game for a bit.

Me: Claire, are you going to get dressed today? It's going to be lunchtime, and you are still running around here with no shirt on.

Claire: Today is "No Shirt Day." I'm dressed already.

Me: Nope, it is not.

Claire: It is. Check your calendar. Then take off your shirt.

Claire: Dad, I want to show you this new thing that was just invented. It's called a "pinky swear."

Me: People have been doing that forever. Probably since they have had pinkies. I bet cave men did pinky swears.

Claire: No. This girl at school just invented it. Let me see your pinky, and I'll show you.

Me: Okay. But it was not just invented.

Claire: Dad, don't ruin it for everyone. Pretend like you've never seen this before. Get surprised.

Claire: Today, in church, we learned about Paul and his friend. They were chained together in prison and still praised the Lord.

Me: You learned about Paul and Silas.

Claire: No, it was Paul and Gladys.

Me: I'm pretty sure it is Paul and Silas.

Claire: No, it is Gladys.

Me: Yeah, you're right. The Apostle Paul was chained to a woman from the 1950s with horn-rimmed glasses.

Claire: Be careful with me. I'm allergic to a lot of things.

Me: You are not allergic to anything.

Claire: Oh, yeah. I feel a cough coming on right now …

Me: That was a burp.

Signs you have been using too much positive reinforcement when bringing up your child.

Claire: That was a wonderful lunch you made. I got this quarter out of my piggy bank just for you.

Me: Ummm … thanks.

Claire: And for driving me to swim lessons, you get this shiny nickel. You keep up the good work, Dad. Remember, you can be anything you want. Keep working hard.

Claire: I finally figured out how to get my shoes on the right feet.

Me: That's great. I was worried you were never going to figure that out. What's your secret?

Claire: I put them on and start walking around. If my feet hurt like crazy, they are on the wrong feet. It's that simple.

Me: A flawless plan.

Claire: For the next couple of days, I will be pretending to be a dog.

Me: Why is that?

Claire: I started kindergarten. At school, I have to pretend to be Claire. I'm running out of time to pretend to be other things.

Me: You know, that's kind of profound. The end of innocence. Will you be starting this now?

Claire: Woof.

Me: Claire, what do you need to do before you put on that new pair of underwear? I think you forgot a step.

Claire: I don't know.

Me: Take off the old ones, silly.

Claire: I thought I might double up. Might get cold tonight.

Car Seat Conversation

Claire: I need to play extra hard when we get home. I have meetings every night this week.

Me: What meeting does a five-year-old have?

Claire: One meeting is about getting more dessert. Another is a vote on Best Dad.

Me: Best Dad?

Claire: Don't worry. We are a team. You got my vote for sure.

Claire: I have really dirty underwear. I need to change them.

Me: You just got home from school. What happened?

Claire: I had to poop at school today. And there was no toilet paper in my stall.

Me: Why didn't you ask for some?

Claire: What am I going to do, walk out in the hallway with no pants and ask for toilet paper? I just pulled them up and went with it.

Me: Learn this phrase: Can you spare a square?

Claire: Dad, what is a vegemeterian?

Me: A person who only eats vegetables. No animals.

Claire: Oh, I could never be that. I could never give up animal crackers.

Me: I'm pretty sure you just put your underwear on backwards.

Kate: The tag is rubbed off on these. Does it really matter?

Me: I guess not. Let's stick with trying to get a leg in each hole.

Kindergarten Homework:

Me: I see a mistake. Every time you write a sentence, you end it with an exclamation point.

Claire: Yes!

Me: We need that to end in a dot. It's called a period.

Claire: No! These clamation points are just those boring dots being happy. It's like they are throwing a little party at the end of my sentence!

Car Seat Conversation

Claire: The juice box you packed me for lunch is the same one my old boyfriend used to like.

Me: What? Five-year-old kindergartners do not have boyfriends!

Claire: Relax, Dad. He was my boyfriend in preschool. It was like forever ago.

Me: Just shoot me now.

Claire: It got cold today.

Me: That is because the seasons are changing. Do you know what season it has become?

Claire: Hot chocolate season.

Claire: Did you know Dora speaks Spanish?

Me: Yes. That is another language. Someday, in school, you will get to learn another language. Do you think you will pick Spanish?

Claire: No. I will pick dog.

Me: I'm afraid that is not a choice.

Claire: Woof.

Claire usually sleeps in while I get up for work at six. This morning, she took my place in bed as soon as I left.

Claire: I got up because you are my best friend, Daddy. And I am yours.

The Better Half (eyes still closed): Hey, I am Daddy's best friend.

Claire (blinking really hard, trying to wink): We'll just let her keep thinking that. She's not even on our team.

Me: Listen, Claire, you cannot toot in public, especially since you're a girl.

Claire: What if one sneaks out of me? Those toots can be real sneaky.

———

Claire: Dad, let me explain something. The kids in kindergarten are in two groups. There are the good kids and the bad kids. I stay away from the bad kids.

Me: I don't think that is good. No one is inherently good or bad. All people are sinners, and all people have the potential for good. Now, who is in your "bad" group?

Claire: Boys.

Me: Forget what I just said. Stay away.

———

Me: What number is this?

Claire: Fiveteen.

Me: You mean fifteen.

Claire: Or fiveteen. I have different names for some numbers.

Me: You got a "needs improvement" on your kindergarten report card for identifying numbers. Know why?

Claire: No. I'm really good. I get every one, like every time.

Me: Like fiveteen out of fiveteen?

Kate: I can't wait to grow up.

Me: Why?

Kate: So I can pee standing up, just like big people. That is my big goal.

Me: About that big goal ...

Claire: I learned all about the presidents today at school.

Me: Oh yeah?

Claire: I know all about George Lincoln now.

Car Seat Conversation

Claire: Dad, a boy at recess was throwing mulch.

Me: So, tell the teacher about it.

Claire: Another boy took care of the situation.

Me: What does that mean? Is there a kindergarten mafia?

Claire: The next time he bent over to grab a handful of mulch, the other boy dumped mulch in his butt. Right in the crack. No more throwing mulch.

Me: Why do you insist on wearing all black and a bandana?

Claire: I'm a special kind of ninja. A Teenage Mutant Ninja Turtle, actually. They are like super new, so you probably don't know about them.

Me: Just like I don't know anything about My Little Pony, Smurfs, Rubik's Cube, Lite Brite ...

———————

Claire: My special class today at school was P.E.

Me: P.E. stands for physical education.

Claire: At my school, it stands for gym.

———————

Tonight, we hosted three college students following an alumni event. Leading to this bedtime conversation:

Claire: I'm kind of sad tonight. One day, I'll leave and go to college. I'll be all alone.

Me: Don't worry. In college, you live in a dorm. It's kind of like a cheap hotel. But you get a roommate.

Claire: I get to pick a roommate? I get a roommate!

Me: Yes.

Claire: Good. I feel so much better. I choose you, Dad. I want you to be my roommate.

Me: I love you, Claire. More than you will ever know.

GONE FISHING

Against all logic, I decided to take Claire fishing. A rite of passage between a father and his kid. I packed a pole, worms, and a little pink tackle box in my SUV. Leaving behind two big tackle boxes, six poles, hip waders, a gaff, and a stringer. All lonely in the back corner of my garage. This was about Claire fishing, and I didn't want to be tempted. I brought my smallest pole for her to use. Next, I carefully explained the dearth of bathrooms at a fishing pond. I made her sit on the potty. Nothing.

Seeing that my smallest pole was twice as tall as Claire, I pulled into the local big box retailer. In the sporting goods aisle, she was immediately drawn to a Barbie-themed pole.

"It lights up when you cast it!" she squealed in delight.

"Goody. A pole guaranteed to break in two casts, light up to scare away any fish, and I will spend more time sitting on the bank taking apart this cheapo Chinese-made reel than fishing," I gruffed as only fathers can.

So, of course, I bought it. That's what you do when you have kids—buy stupid crap you know will break in order to entertain them for seconds at a time. Entire economies of Asian countries depend on this fact. The Barbie pole did come with a tiny net that a guppy could rip through and a little plastic weight, shaped like a fish, to use to practice casting. I feared that weight would be the closest thing to a fish we would see today.

On the way out, the salesman tried to entice me with a "panfish set" of fluorescent plastic lures, just in case we ran into a school of mentally challenged fish that would think these deformed pieces of plastic were food. I was already maxed out on cheap plastic junk for the day. And if those lures worked, I could dig out the heat-deformed Happy Meal toys currently embedded in the back seat of my SUV and fish with those.

I pulled onto the highway and left the city behind us. We were headed to a place where I knew there were fish. Unlike adult men, kids expect to catch fish when fishing.

As soon as we hit the highway, Claire started jabbering away about some TV show with a cartoon cat. She could talk for hours about a twenty-four-minute show. I adjusted the radio until I hit the perfect fade between the front and rear to where I could barely hear her. I kept the "uh-huhs" flowing.

We entered the vast plains where fields of soybeans and corn zipped past. Soon, we pulled into the drive of an old farmhouse. What used to be a gravel driveway had long since lost the battle to clover, and there was no more money for more gravel. We circled the barn, and I could see hand-hewn support posts made from trees that no longer existed in this country. A donkey walked out to say "hi," and Claire squealed with delight. He had two dark stripes across his back in the shape of a cross, and I told her how he is supposed to be the breed that carried Christ to Passover. I prayed that no old lady at church was so into the King James Version of the Bible that Claire started calling the donkey an ass. I was not in the mood for that conversation.

Behind the barn, we found the ideal farm pond. Secluded. Set among fields. The local farmer had mowed the grass along the edges. I loved this place. Claire climbed out of my SUV and wiped her hands down the front of her princess T-shirt. This girl was ready to fish. I vigorously applied sunscreen as though she was a vampire. The FDA states that a child should have a shot glass of sunscreen applied to them. Probably because if you are stuck applying sunscreen to a child, you know exactly how much liquid is in a shot glass. I turned my ball cap around backwards, the international sign that a dude means business. Then I commenced setting up her light-up Barbie pole.

I held Claire's hands in mine, the first cast of her life. Precious. Together, we pushed the button on the back of the pole and flicked the tip toward the water. Barbie jammed, and the hook almost hit me in the face as it came boomeranging back. Unlike every other fisherman in the history of time, I didn't cuss. I just sat down on the bank and started taking the reel apart. Claire started catching grasshoppers in the grass.

The second first cast went almost three feet. Good thing we were at a pond full of fish. I had about as much luck scooping them up with the guppy net. I taught Claire to focus on the red and white bobber.

"When it goes under, pull up and set the hook."

She watched closely, then raised her hand like we were in a classroom. I smiled. My girl had a question about fishing.

"Where are the ducks? Could an otter live here? What if we see a bear? Do rattlesnakes live here?"

"Just watch that bobber."

The bobber went under. Claire stood there. I yelled at her to reel in. The bobber floated to the surface, and she reeled in an empty hook. We did this five times. Those sunfish were sucking down my worms like a free spaghetti dinner. A giant fish jumped up a few feet to the left. Pretty sure I saw it laughing. Maybe it just wanted to see the imbeciles who started a sunfish feeding frenzy while worms needlessly died.

"These fish are so sneaky. Why are fish so sneaky, Daddy?" Claire asked.

While asking, she accidently brought the rod tip of the Barbie pole up and hooked a fish. She started reeling in. The line went slack.

"Oh no! It got off!" said Claire, her eyes welling up.

"Honey, I've lost lots of fish. Sometimes they shake the hook out. Happens to everyone."

Claire put down her pole and started putting things back in the pink tackle box. She picked up the Barbie pole and started walking to the car.

"What are you doing?"

"We might as well leave. That fish is telling all the other fish what we're doing. He knows there is a hook in that worm. Secret is out. We might as well go," she stated.

"It doesn't work like that. You've seen *The Little Mermaid* too many times."

I put another worm on the hook, tossed it in, and handed the pole to Claire. She got the timing and pulled in a sunfish. Then she held it while I took a picture. I could not be more proud.

We threw it in the bucket I brought. She immediately hooked another sunfish. There was a big swirl in the water behind her bobber. Her line tightened, and the Barbie pole started lighting up like a malfunctioning Christmas tree. Claire started screaming. I started screaming. The Barbie pole was bending in half. Claire kept fighting, reeling in a largemouth bass that ate the sunfish she hooked. I grabbed the line to help her pull his big head out of the water. The monster looked at us with disgust, shook his head, and broke the one-pound test line that came with the Barbie pole, then swam off.

I was afraid to turn around. Poor Claire was going to be crushed. I turned slowly.

"Let's catch that fat fish. He's mine," said Claire, sporting the smile of an arsonist.

I loved it.

I saw another swirl in the water. That stupid bass was right by us. I could see him. I snatched a little sunfish from our bucket and popped a hook in his tail. A careful cast dropped it right in the face of the monster bass. I handed the pole to Claire and waited for the action to start. And waited. I could see the bass eyeing the injured sunfish. He turned away. I reeled in the little sunfish, pulled it off the hook, and decided it had been tortured enough to earn freedom. I tossed it back it into the pond. As soon as it broke the surface of the water, the bass engulfed it. Claire and I both stood frozen, wide-eyed.

"See what I mean. Sneaky," she said quietly.

I so wished I had my tackle box so I could use my patented "kitchen sink" technique. This is where I throw every lure I have at a fish and then get mad because I never catch it. I paused. This is about Claire.

I put another worm on Barbie and let Claire do it all alone. Casting and everything. The bobber went under; she pulled up and started reeling in. Perfect. All of a sudden, Barbie lighted up, and the pole was bent over again. Another big bass? She was out-fishing me at my own fishing hole. This thing must have been huge. I put my hands over hers so as not to lose the entire pole. It was as heavy as a log. Bass usually fight and jump. This must have been a catfish.

A moss-covered mass came to the surface. It was a snapping turtle about the size of a car tire with a golden hook in his chin. He was not happy to see us. Claire screamed with glee. I just screamed. I got him close and pulled hard, hoping I had tied a horrible knot to secure the hook. Nope. His tube-sock neck extended toward me. I reached toward him with my needle nose pliers. I was shaking. He was willing to trade the hook for a few fingers. I reached in my back pocket and got out surgical scissors. I had to cut the line as close to the hook as possible, so the big fellow wouldn't get tangled on something under the water and die. The hook would rust out over time.

I got close, and he opened his mouth and hissed. He was going to snatch my whole arm and pull me to a watery death. Poor Claire, she would live as a feral child at this very pond, eating sunfish as her only nourishment. She'd better get that timing down on setting the hook. I snipped the line right next to the hook, and the turtle sunk into the watery depths.

"Easy peasy," I said to Claire while wringing sweat out of my ball cap.

"I want to catch some more. Catch a big one," she said.

"Doesn't get much bigger than that," I said, staring at my still attached fingers.

Claire cast out again but with one hand on her crotch.

"Honey, do you have to go potty? This is why I tried to get you to go before we left."

We ambled over behind my SUV, so she could pop a squat like a true mountain momma. I rummaged through my glove box and came up with one dried out baby wipe. She went pee, and I got her cleaned up, and we returned to fishing.

"I have to go again," she whispered before I could even get a worm on her hook.

We walked back behind my SUV again. She groaned and looked up at me and smiled.

"Are you pooping?" I asked.

A turd the size of a banana appeared. Question answered. New question. How could something so big come out of such a little kid?

"I was going pee-pee, and it just popped out. Once it starts, I can't stop it."

"It's OK. That's how your sister was born."

"Babies are pooped out?"

"Sure," I answered, not wanting to start a whole thing. The Better Half could sort it out later.

I was unsure of what to do next. I didn't have any more wipes. It looked like Claire was going to be riding dirty. The lady who owned the farm was sure to see this giant turd. There was no animal out there that pooped this big. I decided I'd back over her turd when I left, squishing it into the grass, hoping for the best.

The sun started to set, and the sky turned a beautiful pink and orange. The pond became very still. I grabbed my pole and a black jitterbug lure.

"You stand between my arms, and we'll cast out and reel in together," I said as Claire wrapped her tiny hands around mine. Somehow, they fit perfectly. Together, we fished. As a team.

As the jitterbug skimmed across the surface of the pond, the sun dipped below the horizon. I closed my eyes for a long second, trying to commit this to my memory forever. Suddenly, the smooth water exploded. A huge bass ripped the jitterbug. He was hooked. I took a step back, and Claire screamed with glee. She reeled in with all her might. The bass flopped up on the shore next to me. We were both ecstatic.

I removed the hook and showed Claire how to hold a bass right under his lip. She tried, but this fat fish was too heavy for her. I did the holding. I twisted one arm out while holding the huge fish next to her. Somehow, we got a picture. And Claire had the biggest smile I had ever seen. There are two important days to a dad in the life of his daughter: the day she is born and the day she catches her first bass.

As we were driving out, the old lady who owned the pond walked out and let Claire give the donkey a few carrots. We climbed back in the car. Then Claire settled in for a fish-fighting, post-poop nap.

We drove for a while over the plains. It was dark. I pondered "why?" Why do dads do all this? Fighting turtles, poles, and poops. Seems crazy.

I glanced back and saw Claire awake. She silently extended a hand toward me. I reached my hand back toward her. We held hands for a good long while.

That's why.

Claire: I had a real problem at school today.

Me: What was it?

Claire: Kenny was at the water fountain, and I said "3 … 2 … 1 … You're done." And he just kept drinking!

Me: That's not a real problem. You know, there are kids in the world who don't even have water to drink.

Claire: And I know why. Kenny.

Me: Claire, did you just pray for your brother? You don't have a brother.

Claire: I know. I was making sure you were paying attention.

Me: Well, I am.

Claire: Plus, it's a little joke for God. He's all like, "I didn't even give her a brother. Ha! Ha!" Sometimes, God likes a little bit of funny things in our prayers.

Claire: At school today, I went to use the bathroom, and someone had pooped on the seat.

Me: Who did it?

Claire: I don't know. It's a mystery.

Me: You know who could solve it? Encyclopedia BROWN! Get it? Brown.

Claire: Oh, I get it. Not funny.

Me: Hilarious. Dad humor. I'll be performing here the rest of your life. Don't forget to tip your mom.

Claire: Nothing you say makes sense.

Claire: I was trying to read this boy's writing in school, and it was just a line of letters. I said, "You need to start caring about spaces."

Me: Sounds like a rough time.

Claire: Are there jobs where you try to get boys to care about things they don't care about?

Me: Sure. Dietitian, nagging housewife, cardiologist, backseat driver …

Claire: I don't want any of those jobs. Boys are exhausting.

Today we went to the zoo.

Claire: Dad, look at the size of that elephant poop! Wow!

Me: Yes. Very impressive.

Claire: How would you even clean that up? We are NOT getting an elephant.

Me: I'll let Santa know.

Claire and I were watching *Bambi* together.

Me: This part is a little scary. Bambi's mom is going to get shot by a hunter. She will not be coming back.

Claire: Why would a hunter do that?

Me: Some people eat deer. To get food, we kill the animal. It's how we get hamburger and your beloved hot dogs.

Claire: So, to get milk, we take a cow out and shoot it?

Me: Ummm ... no. Not at all. Another scary part is coming up. Everyone is going to get twitterpated.

Claire: What do Chinese people do when they have to cut food?

Me: What?

Claire: Are they just stabbing things with chopsticks all the time?

Me: Did you like the movie?

Claire: Yes.

Me: What was your favorite part?

Claire: The popcorn. It was extra buttery.

When only Claire and Dad go out to eat at a breakfast place for dinner:

Claire: Bet I can eat three of everything. Three pancakes, three eggs, three bacons, three toasts.

Me: I would bet you, but I don't want you to puke.

Claire: I won't puke until we get home. Mom's there.

Me: Sounds like we got a bet.

Claire: What does the word gluttony mean?

Me: Last time I took you to the movies, we sat by a lady who had such a big bucket of popcorn she had to buy a seat for it. It means that.

Claire: Let me finish up these dishes and then I'll help you rake leaves.

Me: Answer truthfully. Are you on drugs?

Claire: We have to get done in time for me to go to the store with Mom. I'm going to be super helpful today.

Me: You're going to kid rehab.

Claire: Did you hear that the flu shot we got was a rip-off?

Me: I think it is ten percent effective. So, you get ten percent.

Claire: I didn't just get ten percent of that needle.

Claire: Dad, if me and you go out to eat, let's ask for a booth.

Me: Okay.

Claire: We will both sit on the same side. We have to. You know why?

Me: Why?

Claire: 'Cause we're a team. And no table can come between us.

Claire: I think I'll be a gym teacher when I grow up.

Me: Why do you say that?

Claire: I'm like the fastest kid in gym. And I jump good. That's probably how they decide who should be a gym teacher.

Claire: Dad, I think I might go to your college one day.

The Better Half: What about mine?

Claire: Didn't all your college friends become doctors and lawyers?

The Better Half: Yeah.

Claire: No thanks. I'm not a nerd.

Claire looking over my shoulder at the drink menu at a local restaurant.

Claire: I think you should get a craft beer. That sounds really fun.

Me: That is not a beer that comes with glitter, glue, and scissors.

Claire: Oh. Get whatever you want then.

We visited a farm. We saw a huge pig lying in some grass under a doorway.

Claire: I bet his name is Wilbur, and a friendly spider will save him.

Me: I bet his name is bacon.

Claire: Mom showed me this book. And in it, babies don't come out of a mommy's belly; they come out the CROTCH!

Me: You're kidding!

Claire: No. I'm being true. This is blowing my mind. But don't tell anyone. Mom wants to keep our talk a secret. I'm just telling you because we are a team.

Me: Don't worry. Your secret is safe with me.

Claire: I have a specially needed kid in my class at school.

Me: What do you think "specially needed" means?

Claire: That we need them. Especially. Am I wrong?

Me: You are right. So right.

Me: How was school today?

Claire: Horrible. We had "the talk." I have a Virginia. What is sex?

Me: I brought home some cookies. Let's eat cookies and forget this whole thing ever happened.

NEXT MAN UP

There is a long-standing tradition among the presidents, supposedly started by George Washington. The outgoing president clears everything from the Oval Office, leaving one item. In the top drawer of the president's desk is a handwritten letter for the incoming president. Only the two of them can understand the impossible job one is leaving and the other is undertaking. One is coming in looking young and spry while the outgoing president needs a cane and Depends. The presidency ages them at an incredible rate. Just like the job my successor will inherit. Welcome to parenthood.

I do not plan on my term as The First Dad ending anytime soon. But I have recently been reminded that life is unpredictable. My term as Dad has not always gone smoothly. I may have tried to sway my constituents with too many sweets, and not monitored screen time enough in that anything made in the 1980s was automatically acceptable, even if in the show Michael J. Fox tried to sleep with his mom or Luke Skywalker made out with his sister. But overall, this work has been the delight of my life.

Just in case of an unforeseen tragedy, and I am forced from office, I wanted to leave some advice to my successor. I write this in the manner of a presidential letter:

Dear Number Two,

That reference is not intended as a poop joke. I am just stating that you are the second dad, but you might want to get used to poop jokes. If your constituents ever ask you to play twenty questions, just lead with, "I'd like to guess the object. A turd." Game over.

You are about to embark on a journey. The days will be long and the years short. But there is a joy in this journey. Sometimes, you have to work to find it, but it is there. I am entrusting you to pick up where I left off. I have multiple pieces of advice for you, Dad Number Two.

First ... sorry I bought those two miniature snow shovels in the garage. They seemed like a delightful idea at the time. Your constituents, though, prefer to use them to transport the snow you shovel off the driveway back onto the driveway. There is a wooden corncob pipe and buttons in the garage by the lawnmower. Your constituents will want to a build a snowman. Within fifteen seconds, they will both get snow in their mittens and start crying that it is too cold. They will go inside and watch you build the snowman from the picture window. While drinking hot chocolate. Neighbors will drive by and wave, wondering why a grown man is building a snowman in his front yard. Alone.

We have a huge sectional in the living room. My spot is in the far corner. That is now your spot. When you get up to get a drink, two little girls will jump into your place and start laughing like a pair of hyenas. You will have to pretend not to see or hear them when you return and slowly sit on them. They will find this absolutely hilarious.

Speaking of drinking, I leave you the mini fridge in the basement. It is full of hard cider and girly drinks. As much as I tried, I never got much of a taste for beer. I get *The New Yorker* magazine every week. Read it. Try to stay mentally nimble or full of girly drinks. No in between. The three females in the household will dominate you. Regardless. Might as well either have your senses about you or none at all.

I do all the grocery shopping and almost all the cooking. Coupons are in the left-hand drawer of the china hutch, and don't get me started on why we have a cabinet of expensive plates we never use.

Your new chief of staff wants us to eat like we are Paleo-Vegans. Your two constituents want to eat like it is a birthday party during Mardi Gras. Good luck navigating that.

You are inheriting a fat female goldendoodle. She is our second goldendoodle. She will never love you like she loved me. Just accept it. I did have a talk with her about not biting you. We agreed she would only bite you a little bit.

I leave you all my fishing gear in the garage. If you don't fish, start. But if you catch bigger fish than I caught, I swear I will haunt you. Not in a Casper way. In a Poltergeist way. So, take up the hobby of fishing and just catch the little ones.

One of your constituents sleeps like your new chief of staff. Dead to the world in ten seconds. The other sleeps like me. Terribly. She will lie down for five minutes, get out of bed in tears, and tell you she had a horrible nightmare. She will go into great detail telling you about this dreadful dream that she most certainly did not have. It is quite scary. Then you won't be able to sleep either. You will know which constituent this is after the first night.

About your new chief of staff, she's great. Really great. And you don't deserve her, just like I didn't. She's the real president, by the way. Don't ever kid yourself about that. She is kind, hardworking, and really good at making lists of things that need to be done. I do have a few tips on keeping things harmonious.

Pretend the Essential Oils work. We all know they are bogus. In her heart of hearts, your new chief of staff knows it too. But if you get the flu, after she puts some ginger, rosemary, cucumber combination across your forehead like the priest anointing the little girl in *The Exorcist*, say, "I feel better already." And ignore the oils as a line item in the budget. She offsets enough of the cost by selling them to her gullible friends who did not pay attention in junior high science when a concept called The Scientific Method was taught.

The chief of staff pretends to love movies. Always let her pick what you watch. She'll pick some dumb Hallmark Christmas lovefest despite it being July. When she lies on the couch with the tan pillow under her head and the purple blanket on her feet, it's over. She's asleep in two minutes, and you can watch robots fight each other. When you wake her to go up to bed, just say her movie ended with the new guy in town finally getting together with the lady with the failing Christmas tree business. Turns out, he was an unemployed lumberjack, and it was a match made in heaven. Riveting.

Your new chief of staff is a lawyer. Her arguments are essentially the defensive line of the 1985 Chicago Bears. For instance, she wanted to get some monstrosity of a playset and a giant trampoline for the backyard. I argued that we had a wonderful playground at the end of our block. I also brought forth evidence that trampolines lead to injury and a rise in insurance costs. Enjoy mowing the backyard. There is a gigantic playset and a trampoline back there.

You are inheriting a great house. Everything on the inside and outside is new. We bought the house when we were first married because we liked everything and wouldn't have to change anything. We have since changed every single thing. Your new chief of staff probably failed to disclose that her parents rebuilt their house from the ground up, and even below the ground, in that they jacked up the house and added a basement with a fireplace in it. You are destined for more of the same.

Your new father-in-law did all that work. Tools to me are like a bicycle to a fish. So, like the much-maligned Hallmark movies, I hope you are a construction worker who builds houses by hand or a contractor who likes to work for free and getting together with her is destiny. Bad news: Don't get too attached to anything in the house, including the walls. In two years, she's changing all of it. Good news: I won't be haunting you. In a couple years, the house will look so different that this ghost won't be able to find it.

Bottom line, your new chief of staff is amazing. Loyal. Kind. And if you get in some horrible accident and all you can do is blink your left eye to communicate, she'll spend the rest of her life caring for you. And that is what you want.

Your oldest constituent is a girl named Claire. She exudes empathy. All you need to do is encourage her and get out of her way. She is definitely an old soul. This may be because she thinks she is a dog, and that would make her like seventy years old in dog years.

Work hard to bond with Claire. At some point, at a very young age, Claire declared that she and I were a "team" and we always would be. Being on Claire's team has been one of the greatest pleasures of my life.

Claire is super creative. While other kids were building basic houses out of Legos, she was building Santa's workshop with electric lighting. Seriously.

If you get sick, Claire will take care of you. When you get old, she will be the one calling every day to check on you. When you end up in a nursing home, she'll be there to cut your Jell-O with a spork and to listen to you rant about flipping through the Sears Catalog Wish Book looking for Christmas presents in 1984. Once you are a team with Claire, you're a team forever.

I hope you like movies about dogs. Because Claire does. A lot. Remember a movie called *Air Bud*, about a golden retriever who plays basketball? Those people started their own Air Bud production company, and they make talking dog movies. And there are a lot of them. You will spend many Saturday nights with Air Bud.

Claire plays piano, loves to draw, and is inherently good at math. At her first-grade parent-teacher conference, the teacher ended with a list of adjectives like helpful, kind, and caring. She circled ones that the student should work on to improve. Claire was her only student where she had none to circle. Our babysitter said she was the nicest kid she ever watched. And she watched a lot of kids.

Your last constituent is Kate. Claire will take care of you every day in old age, but in the end, Kate will have the guts to pull the plug on your life support. You need both constituents in your presidency. If Kate likes you, she will let you know. If she doesn't like you, you will know right away, because she will kill you.

A couple of things about Kate: She could become the president. Of our country. And she'd be a dang good one. And she'll become president of your house if you let her. She is a master negotiator. Every meal includes a "deal" for dessert, every chore turns into a chore you can end up doing, as she "teaches" you how to do it. She is wicked smart. She is frank at all times. Gain weight, she'll let you know. Wear brown scuffed-up shoes to church, and she'll tell you that you are wearing "turds" in God's house.

At two, Kate was correcting my driving directions from a backwards facing car seat. At three, she was stacking plastic IKEA chairs to make ladders to get everything we had placed above her reach. She is capable of memorizing anything she sees or hears. Double check that you have the Christian radio station on when you get in the car, or the dirtiest pop song you ever heard will be sung back to you, word for word, for a week.

In college, you might have had a friend who drank until he puked, over and over again. This is Kate, but instead of abusing alcohol, she can't quit the sugar. When she goes to a birthday party, she convinces the host to give her two pieces of frosting laden cake while the other kids get one. Then she'll use her brown hair and brown eye combination to get Tommy to give her his cake. Next thing you know, she's puking in the car on the way home. A week later, at a different birthday party, you see her digging into a third piece of birthday cake, and she looks up at you and smiles, those brown eyes sparkling, and you both know what is next. She's puking all the way home.

One time at a birthday party, a pleasant chief of staff from another household asked if Kate could come home with and her daughter for a sleepover. She was dutifully warned that Kate probably had too much cake and her car's interior was at risk. The mom smiled and said, "I'm sure it will be fine."

It was fine all right. Fine all over her car before they even got out of the driveway. I don't feel bad. She had fair warning.

If Kate gets caffeine, she's a straight-up evil Gremlin. Seriously.

Claire will care for you when you're old. Kate will invent the medical device that saves your life. Claire saves the world through love. Kate plans on fixing the world through dogged determination.

I leave you with a household in a good place. There is always work to be done, according to the handwritten lists of the chief of staff—also known as The Better Half—but we are trending up. Continue my work of loving The Better Half despite her being a lawyer, convincing constituent Claire that being the proprietor of a hotel for dogs is not actually a career, and making Kate hold hands with Claire while crossing the street without thinking of it as an opportunity to slingshot her sister into traffic.

You see, Dad Number Two, all of this almost didn't happen. After Claire was born, a deep sadness encompassed me. It was crushing. I needed help. Baby Claire was ruining my life. I was sinking. Drowning.

At the last possible moment, something reached through the murky darkness. It was not the muscular arm you are probably thinking of. No caped crusader to the rescue. It was a simple smile. A tiny, sweet grin from baby Claire. It was the smile that a baby girl reserves for her daddy.

In an instant, I saw that same smile as she said "Dada" for the first time.

That smile as she took her first awkward steps into my outstretched arms.

That smile as she saw her first snow and I ran around the backyard with her in my arms teaching her how to catch snowflakes on her tongue.

That smile as I helped her pull her first tooth and saw the new gap in that smile.

That smile when I snuck a hamster under the tree on Christmas morning.

That smile as I picked her up after her first day of kindergarten. We held hands all the way home as she told me she missed me all day.

That smile as I let go of the back of her bike seat and we both screamed as she rode down the street for the first time.

I saw it graduate high school.

Then college.

That smile waiting for me to walk her down an aisle.

That smile holding her own baby.

That smile saying goodbye to me as I leave this life to go see my red dog with the wagging tail.

I was hopeless and helpless. I blamed baby Claire. And in return, she smiled and made us a team. Forever.

Claire: I'm working on whistling. I know it just sounds like breathing, but I'm practicing.

Me: Keep practicing. You will get it. You can do anything you put your mind to.

Claire: Thanks. Me and you are a team, Dad. Even when I was a little baby. It was always me and you.

Me: I wish that were true. There was a time when I didn't want to be on any team. Thinking of it makes me sad. I'm so sorry.

Claire puts her face right next to mine. Our eyeballs almost touching.

Claire: Me and you. We're a team.

Me: Being on your team is the best thing that ever happened to me. You saved me.

Author Bio

Jon Woolley has been a classroom teacher for over 25 years. He thought he knew children—until he had two of his own. His education degrees didn't help much when his youngest daughter was accidentally born on the bathroom floor.

Jon's work has appeared in *The Writing Disorder, Come on Georgia*, and his humorous essay, "Record Low," was published in *The Columbus Dispatch*.

A former Division I basketball player, Jon is now exactly 80 inches tall for no reason. He lives in Columbus, Ohio, with his lawyer wife and is often the primary caregiver for their two daughters. They are the reason he writes.

Follow Jon Woolley

Website: jonwoolleyauthor.com
Facebook: Carseat Conversations
Instagram: @carseatconversations
Podcast: Writing in Progress

www.ingramcontent.com/pod-product-compliance
Lightning Source LLC
LaVergne TN
LVHW011930070526
838202LV00054B/4572